COLLECTION OF

47 SCARY
AND
UNEXPLAINABLE
STORIES

COLLECTION OF

47 SCARY

AND

UNEXPLAINABLE

STORIES

ELIAS CAMACHO

COLLECTION OF 47
SCARY AND UNEXPLAINABLE
STORIES

iUniverse books may be ordered through booksellers or by contacting:

iUniverse
1663 Liberty Drive
Bloomington, IN 47403
www.iuniverse.com
844-349-9409

ISBN: 978-1-6632-3670-8 (sc)
ISBN: 978-1-6632-3678-4 (e)

Print information available on the last page.

iUniverse rev. date: 03/15/2022

CONTENTS

I dedicate this book to my Grandmother
Natalia Araiza and my mother Luz.

PREFACE

I don't think there is a person alive who at one time or another has not heard a ghostly story. And there are many of us who have our own ghost story to tell. There is something to say about being scared. To have that cold feeling, tingling sensation on your arms and neck and your blood rushing up to your head, a chill running down your spine, goose bumps a shortness of breath, and a focus concentration on details.

It's really something amazing and thrilling, and we love it. Let's face it, we like being scared, no doubt about it. What would a campfire or a sleep over be without a scary story?

We are intrigued with things that make us feel vulnerable and love that feeling of being scared, so much that the entertainment industry has made a large profit out of scaring us. Movie after movie comes out every year and each trying to outdo the other and now with special affects its even greater. The unexplainable has become so popular lately that a couple of TV shows have come out with stories based on individual experiences to activities including whole buildings and towns who seem to be possessed, and they are enjoying great ratings. Of course, not all stories are frightful to a degree of hysteria, some just simply can't be explained and leave the person in a state of wonder and bewilderment.

There are basically 3 ways these type of stories have survived through the years. The most common is probably the ones that are handled down from generation to generation, by word of mouth.

Those that are in print and now those who are on film. There is a tendency of some stories to change through time to fit the occasion. But non the less they are based on something.

But when it comes to entertainment, obviously some of these movies are made up, and some stories are exaggerated, all to make a bigger impact. And even those that are not, sometimes they are so out of the norm that they are hard to believe. But not believing, in certain ways is not unusual, very often even the affected person wonders if it in fact it happened. They wonder if in fact they saw what they think they saw or heard what they think they heard and all because of the traumatic and unusual nature of the event

And then there are those stories that are told and repeated to relay a message from one generation to the next while others are just simply something that happened to someone and due to its nature are retold over and over again. Some are even meant to teach us a lesson of some sorts. Some stories have been around for generations and its origins lost to time. Yet others occurred yesterday. Everyday new stories come to being, and new stories are told. Either way we try to make reason and explain the event itself or the reason for the event so we can make sense of it.

While growing up I heard my share of ghostly stories. Some of them were pure bull and made up, especially when a bunch of us pre-teens would get together at night at the corner and try to outdo each other. I can't recall any of them anymore I guess because they were made up as we went along.

But yet there are those stories that have remained with me too this date. Especially those told to me by respectable grown-ups and people I looked up to. They had a great impact on me. Regardless if the intent was to impress or teach me something at the time, the impact of these stories was there and has remained, and in many instances, have made a change in my behavior and the way I look at things. There were those stories that were told to us by friends and there were those told to us by strangers and then there were those that were told to us by family members such as parents and grandparents each carried its special merits.

Cause let's face it, for the most part, many of the stories that were told to us as children were intended to give us some kind of a message, or a lesson especially coming from parents, educators, and clergy. Even if all were not true in nature, they at least had some fact behind it. These stories were supposed to cause some type of change or confirmation in our behavior and our way of looking at life. They were kind of a reality check and/or a behavior adjustment, may it be spiritual, moral, social, or whatever.

Most of the stories that I heard, surprisingly enough were things that happen too many of my relatives or acquaintances. And even though in some cases some of the main characters I didn't personally know, it still carried weight. This in itself, made them even more realistic, amazing, and believable and had a bigger impact on me. They caused such a significant effect on me knowing that they came from someone I knew and respected. If it happened to them, it surely had to be true, and it could happen to me. Knowing the person who experienced the event gave it more validity, and there was no doubt in my mind that it did happen. Whatever it was that caused that event, I for sure was going to do whatever was necessary to avoid from experiencing the same thing.

As I got older, I would often think of some of these stories that I had heard as a youngster and a part of me would often wonder if in fact, these stories were actually true. Life experiences had now caused me to question the event. I mean, did they really happen? Why did they happen? How rational does it sound? Was it logical? Especially when there was no fault or action taken by the victim, to have caused them to have experienced such an event?

Of course, not all events are scary; some of them are just simply things that happened that are just not explainable, but yet well out of the ordinary and strange. They are just simply matter-of fact type of stories. Nevertheless, they leave you bewildered.

One thing I recalled later was that in none of the events was anybody really hurt. I mean, whatever happened just scared or left the person thinking but there was no physical harm. With some exceptions of course. The event was just to scare you or cause you to change direction and no real physical harm came out of it. Of course, there were those rare occasions where someone did suffer physical harm and even death.

It was not until some years later when some strange unexplainable things happened to me that I realized that in fact some of these stories could very well be true. Or at least the probability was there. When I tell people some of the stories or things that happened to me, I often can sense the skepticism. And I can't blame them; it's sometimes hard to believe some of these stories. They usually keep staring at me waiting for me to smile or laugh, waiting for the punch line, you might say. The same thing is not true when I tell these stories to my grandchildren, they believe every word I say. There is something to say about innocence.

I'm not so naïve that I don't know that throughout the ages diverse cultures have produced stories that were meant to build character, especially to their young. These stories would always have a strong message, which was intended to alter or maintain a certain control over the young ones. These stories would enable parents to keep their kids in line and set an orderly natural rhythm to human behavior acceptable to society. The young would learn at an early age the proper way to conduct themselves among their peers and seniors and society as a whole and they would also learn the consequences of improper behavior.

Even Jesus used parables to teach things to his disciples and followers, so it's nothing new. And it's also quite understandable why some generations and society as a whole would have a need for some stories. However not all stories are meant to accomplish a task, some really have no lesson to learn. In certain cases, it's just something that occurred, something unexplainable outside of the norm to where we can call them paranormal.

One day I started to wonder just how many people had ever

experienced any scary or unexplainable events like I did. Or if this type of events only happened to certain people and others go through life without ever experiencing anything like this.

I wondered, how rampant are these stories? So, at every opportunity I started asking people that I met or that I know if they had ever had an experience with something scary or unexplainable, not necessarily paranormal, just something that can't be explained. I preferred that it be something that actually happened to them. Or at least to someone who they knew personally and trusted and who they could believe.

To my amazement and surprise, I found out that mostly everyone at one time or another has had some type of experience with something that they can't explain. Sometimes, the event was something that can even be considered as supernatural or paranormal. Many of the people telling me these stories were persons that I have known for years or were related and who had never mentioned the event to anyone before. They just tried to go on as if nothing had happened. Mostly all of them, ether did not like thinking about what happened or they felt no one would believe them, or no one had ever asked them.

It was so amazing to hear story after story, such that I decided to collect these stories and include them in this book. I know that most of these stories are true because I know the people to whom the incident occurred too or the person telling me the story. I got more stories then what I had expected and some I didn't include because I had my doubts. The ones I did include, well, I'm sure they wouldn't make them up, and yet, well, you be the judge and by the way how does it compare to YOUR story?

INTRODUCTION

I come from a very large family. There were eleven siblings at home, and we had countless of uncles, aunts, and cousins. Very typical Mexican. We were also very close to my maternal grandmother who lived with us. Our circle of acquaintances included all the kids in the neighborhood, who were many.

My neighborhood was a traditional Mexican neighborhood, and, in those days, people would gather in the evenings outside their homes and talk. It was not unusual for someone to be passing by and stopping to cheat for a while. Everybody knew everybody in the neighborhood.

I was about 8 years when I first saw a Television set. They were so expensive we didn't have one till my pre-teen years and that was the case for most of us living in the Val Verde neighborhood at the time, most of us would either listen to the radio or hang out, especially in the evening and there was a lot of time for conversations.

It was here, during this time that a lot of stories were told. Most of the stories that I personally knew growing up came from my grandmother Natalia Araiza. I spend a lot of time with my grandmother as a child and she was actually the one who thought me how to pray and how to properly behave. She would take me to church in the morning for Mass and to the rosary in the evening. I was so brain washed (not really, I liked it) at the time that I became an Altar Boy when I was eight years old. Most of the stories that my grandmother told me were when I was between the ages of eight and eleven. By the age of twelfth I was already in junior High and started to drift away from grandma and the church, but many of these stores stayed on in the back on my mind.

But grandma was not the only person that told me and my other siblings some of these stories. I also heard stories from my mom (Luz) and dad (Demecio) and other older relatives that would frequently visit our house. Relatives like Manuel Rosales a cousin of my mother who would later die in an accident when the truck he was driving overturned and rolled over him. There were also other stories that came from people like our local parish priest Father Juan Zelaya, my uncle Pete, and my uncle Gonzalo. Some of the stories I have since forgotten, but others have stayed with me. I must say that many of these stories at the time, put the fear of God in me when I was smaller. There were many things that I would have probably done or NOT done had it not been for some of these stories.

But not only did I hear stories in my youth, but later on in life as well. From people like my Father-in-law and my wife's uncle Rodolfo and even my own wife. Surprisingly enough in later years I would even hear stories from my own children.

I recall once when I was a teenager asking my mom of how come most of these stories seemed to have occurred in the *Old Days*. I recall my mom telling me that it was simple. My mom told me that in this world there was a constant struggle between good and evil.

That God was the good and the Devil was the evil. That the devil was constantly competing with God and trying to take souls away from God and take them with him to hell. By doing this the Devil was trying to show God that he was more powerful and could take more souls then God. And besides, in the old days people were more religious, more God fearing and more kind to each other. People in those days would always be trying to help each other out. People kept their word and did unto others as they wanted others to do unto them. Kids would mind their parents, have respect for others and would in general behave. Thus, things being the way they were, the devil would always be trying to trick people into doing bad things, because people were generally good. The devil would lie and con people into evil conduct. The devil would continue to work on these souls making them to do bad things until one day he would take their soul. The devil was constantly appearing to people, but always in disguise. Seldom did the Devil appear to people in his true nature because people would freak out. Just like the devil appeared to Adam and Eve disguised as a snake and lied to them. That's what the Devil had to do in those *older days,* mislead and fool people my mom said.

Why doesn't the devil appear to people now n days anymore? I would ask Mom. Because he doesn't have too, people now in days are devils themselves my mom would say. People are no longer afraid of the Devil. The way people live their lives, cheating, lying, stealing, and breaking every Commandment that God has given us. Now the devil's job is easy. He doesn't have to worry about coming out and lying and tricking people. People are now doing so many terrible things that they are doing the Devil's job and getting in line by themselves to go to hell.

Mom once told me that many of these appearing souls (ghost) were lost souls, which were in limbo, meaning that they were neither in hell nor in haven. These souls had been allowed to continue here on earth until they finish a particular task or make penance for some bad deed. These souls would sometimes require the assistance of a living person. Mom said that these souls would eventual complete their passage into the other world. I also remember my mom telling me that I should never worry or fear these ghosts and other dead people. That they would never hurt me, that it was the people who were **alive**, whom I should fear and worry about because they were the ones who could mislead me and hurt me.

My mom and my grandmother are gone now, but I can look around in our society now and days and see what they meant. God no longer has a place in our lives. Not in our personal life's and not in society's life. What used to be Good is now Bad and what used to be Bad is now Good.

The way people use our Constitution to separate Church and State has gone beyond what our forefathers intended, at least, that's my opinion. Growing up we used to pray in school in the morning and before all sporting events. This was true regardless, if the event was a formal or non-formal events. It just seemed like the right thing to do. And the prayer was not to win, but simple to stay healthy and for no one to get hurt. And this was meant for our team as well as the other team.

Now in days you read every day in the newspapers were someone with the help of the civil liberty union has filed a lawsuit because of this and that trying to have courts and law makers change things to their singular way of thinking. Oh my God! Have we gone too far? There was even a lawsuit in a city in New Mexico named Las Cruces (the crosses) because the city government used the symbol of three crosses in their official dealings. The petitioners were saying that the crosses (a simple of Christianity) was offensive (to those non-Christian believers) and against the Constitution. At that rate, it won't be long before we will have to change the names of most of our cities like Los Angles, San Francisco, Saint Luis, San Antonio and so forth. These are names of Saints, and I guess there is a conflict between Church and State in these cases as well.

There is also a metal cross close by to San Diego overlooking the Pacific Ocean which has been there for over eighty years as a monument for our servicemen. This monument will probably have to come down because someone thought it violated their non-religious rights. What about the school that took out the word "Christ" from Silent Night which we all sing in Christmas? And the courthouse that was made to remove a plaque that had the Ten Commandments' from in front of the courthouse.

In January 2014 the Associated Press came out with a story of a satanic group who had unveiled designs for a 7-foot-tall, goat-headed deity that it wanted to place at the Oklahoma's State Capitol. All because the Satanic Temple said Oklahoma's decision to put a Ten Commandments monument at the Capitol, had opened the door for their statute, this due to equal rights. The design featured a horned demon sitting in a pentagram-adorned throne with children next to it. All in the name of civil rights!

In my opinion, when it comes to religion and the supernatural, the Church has kept pretty quiet, to quite if you ask me. Although the church makes it obvious that the supernatural, body possessions, witchcraft, shamanism, and various other forms of diabolical events and phenomena do exist and are true, the church is pretty much silence about the subject. It seems that the Church as a whole does not like to go public about these matters and it is very careful as to what it says.

It seems to me that this could be due to what took place in the early centuries of the church. Before mental illness was accepted as behavioral condition, the church was part of an unintentional conspiracy to condemn many mentally ill persons because it was believed that evil spirits had possessed them. It was believed that people acted the way they did because of these evil spirt possessions.

There were also many innocent women (and man) that were burned because it was believed they were witches who practiced and worshiped the devil. (Although it much be accepted that in fact there were some) Superstitions, fear and ignorance caused much mayhem in many parts of the world in those days, and many innocent people suffered for it. Not until the medical profession was able to ascertain that in fact mental illness was the main cause of many peoples irregular behavior did the church cease its persecutions.

Maybe it's because of this fact, that it has now caused the church to first look at other factors for the irregular behavior of a person, such as mental illness and other physical ailments that can be causing the behavior.

The person's culture is also taken into consideration when addressing these matters. The church wants to address all of these factors before looking at the spiritual and supernatural.

There are many booklets for prayers to combat diabolical fears and possible possessions or influences.

Booklets such as "Spiritual Warfare Prayers," (United States Catholic Conference) "Healing Power Prayers" and many more that can be obtained through the internet or in certain religious stores or churches. So obviously, the Church does believe in this type of activity, only it keeps it on a low profile. There is no doubt that evil does exist.

A few years ago, I attended a seminar given by Fr. Robert Dueweke, OSA, PH.D of the Tepeyac Institute in which he spoke of Witchcraft, Shamanism, and healing in the Catholic Church. Father Dueweke lived in Peru for 15 years and worked very closely with a Curandero (Healer). The culture in Peru (as well as other Latin American countries) is such that a person believes in witchcraft from a very young age. There is also a great faith and trust in the healing power of a Curandero. Although the Curandero mainly cures body ailments with herbs, it is not uncommon for them to go beyond that, as many claim to have great psychic powers. They will use material things such as holy water, candles, religious pictures and other religious statues besides prayers and herbs. A Curandero is not only seen as a healer of the body, but of the spirt as well.

In most Latin countries a priest is called a "Cura" which means healer. The word "andero" means a wonderer or traveler, hence "Curandero" A healer who travels.

So, in a matter of speaking, a priest can be considered a healer, (of the faith) who travels. Saint Luke who is well known in the Catholic religion as the Doctor of the church and is looked at as a Curandero. St. Luke used herbs to heal people and did wonders healing people before becoming one of Jesus Disciples.

Later on, once he became an apostle and after Jesus death (after receiving the holy spirt, as Catholics believe the apostles did) he was able extent his abilities as a healer to include fighting the supernatural and conducting miracles. So not only did he fight the body deceases but the spirt as well. So, I guess we can see how a Curandero can also be construed be a healer of body and spirt and many faithful have faith and a great trust in the Curanderos.

The important thing to remember is that these Curanderos, white witches, or whatever you want to call them, when they are true healers, and believers in the faith, there main concern is to help the individual and society as a whole. They are not in to obtain any personal financial gain. They will not have store fronts with flashing neon lights and such. You will usually only find them through word of mouth. And if you want to offer or give a gratuity for their services many will usually accept it, but it's really up to you they will not ask for it.

The seminar was very interesting and shined light on many things that I have always wondered about or have had doubts. Due to the extent and nature of the subject I will not go into it in any more depth now but let me tell you that I came out of the seminar believing that there are certain things that happen in this world that nobody can explain and there are more occurrences then one knows.

One thing no one has to tell us, because all of us have at one time or another have experience it, is that there is GOOD and EVIL in this world. And there is also people who practice one or the other. But when it comes to Evil, one must have faith and believe that if you believe in our lord, nothing can harm you, because he is more powerful that anything in this whole universe. At least this is what the catholic faith teaches us.

Anyway, all of this would be material for a different subject or book. For now, let's just look at the stories of unexplainable things and scary events that I have been able to collect. There are many stories that I did not include because of certain doubts that I had.

In the ones that I did include I will give you short synopsis or little explanation as to where that story came from. You can be the judge if it's true or not. I am simply telling you what I was told and the way I was told. But, rest a sure that there had to have been some bases for the story.

STORY 1

THE ALTAR BOY

Father Juan Celaya arrived at Our Lady of the Light Catholic Church in the mid 1950's. The church was located on Dolan Street, and it was a short walk to our house. Padre Juan (as everyone called him) was our parish priest and he took his job very serious and saw our neighborhood and its people as his flock.

As I mentioned before our neighborhood was prominent Hispanic, and all the families were lower middle income, and it was not unusual to have two or three generations living in the same household. With very few exceptions, the whole neighborhood attended Our Lady of the Light Church, and everyone knew everyone.

I was one of about a dozen or so Alter boys who assisted Father Juan at the church. Our ages ranged from about 9 to 14. Mass (church services) was in Latin in those days, and we had regular training sessions to make sure we knew our prayers in Latin. Father Juan did the training and as part of the training he would also explain to us the parts of the Mass and for what they stood for. When time permitted Father Juan would also tell us Bible stories and explain to us what the stories meant. Father Juan would also answer and explain any questions or doubts that we might have.

On one occasion I remember Father Juan telling us a story about an Altar Boy who lived some years ago. According to Father Juan this Altar boy was the epitome of an altar server. He was always early to church. He was friendly, helpful, and kind to everyone. He did everything that was expected of him, and he was well loved by all.

This boy suddenly became ill one day and passed away without the local priest having time to give him his last rites. The local priest thought so highly of this Altar boy that he obtained special permission from the bishop to bury the boy next to the church in holy ground.

It wasn't long before the priest started to hear people mention that they had seen the dead altar boy in the church at various times. Each time that he was seen, the boy was in a praying position close to the Altar. But the priest had never seen him. After a while even some of the Altar boys claimed to have seen the boy as well. The dead Altar boy's apparitions usually didn't last long.

One morning while preparing for the daily Mass and being by himself, the priest happened to see the dead Altar boy. The dead boy was kneeling by the Altar praying. The priest approached the dead boy and asked him why he was there and if there was anything he could do for him. The dead Altar boy replied "yes." The dead Altar boy told the priest that he needed for his human remains to be removed from holy ground. The boy told the priest that he had never made a good and honest confession while alive and didn't deserve to be buried in Holy ground.

Shortly after that, the dead Altar boys remains were unearthed and removed to a common cemetery.

For a very long time after hearing this story I was always afraid to be in the church by myself. I hated it when I was the last one to leave and had to turn the lights off inside the big church.

I was always afraid that I was going to see the dead Altar boy somewhere in the church. Not only that but we also served as Altar boys in funerals, and I had served mass for a lot of the dead and always wondered if anyone of them might appear to me.

And needless to say, I was always very conscientious whenever I went to confession.

STORY 2

THE GRAVE DIGGER

The house in which I was raised had three main rooms and to one side my parents had added three more smaller ones. This rooms and had been built adjacent to an old irrigation ditch which was no longer used but remnants were still there. These rooms which were made out of adobe were separated from the main house by a porch which ran in-between. For the most part, we kids (there were eleven of us) slept in these rooms, which in the inside instead of doors had curtains.(doors were added later on) Some of us slept 2-3 per bed.

I remember sleeping in the middle room until my older brother Beto got married and moved out of the house. Beto was six years older than me. The girls slept in one room and the boys in the other.

When I was around nine or ten I (1955-1956) I recall being sick one night and having a fever. During the night I heard some noises coming from outside of the window which faced the old irrigation ditch. The sound was a swishing sound like when a shovel digs into the ground. The sound went on for a while and I got up to looked out the window. I saw a person digging a hole standing in the middle of where the ditch used to be. Due to the darkness, I couldn't make out any physical characteristics of the person, but I was sure it was a man who was wearing a long black overcoat and a hat. It was a cold windy night and there was some slight rain falling. This

3

frighten the daylights out of me, so I went back to bed, covered my head and prayed till I finally fell asleep. For some unknown reason I never thought at the time about telling someone or calling out to my parents.

I never told anyone of this occurrence, and I did think about it on occasions. But, as I got older, I explained the occurrence to myself as an imagination due to the fever which caused me to see things, and besides with time I wasn't really sure if I had actually seen something or not.

In February 2014 while having dinner with my siblings I happen to be seating next to my brother Beto and during the evening I told him of this book I was writing. I asked Beto if he had any scary or unexplainable stories that he had experience that I could use in my book. After a few minutes Beto said, yea, I have one.

Beto went on to say that one night while growing up in the old house, he had heard some noise coming from outside the window while he was asleep. Beto said he was around thirteen or fourteen years old at the time. I asked Beto which bedroom and he said, "the one in the middle." Beto said the noise was like when a shovel goes into the dirt.

I thought, oh shit!. Beto continued saying that after hearing this for a while, he got up and looked out the window. Beto said he then saw an old man digging a hole and the old man turned to look at Beto and pointed his finger as if indicating it was for him. Beto jumped back into bed and prayed all night long until he fell to sleep.

The next day thinking it was a dream he disregarded what he had seen. However, the following night again he heard the same noise and again he looked out the window and saw the same old man and again the old man pointed his finger at Beto. Beto said this went on for three nights and on the fourth day, during daylight he went outside to the area, where he had seen the individual and he sat there thinking and looking at the ground. Beto said he kept looking at the area trying to figure out what the hell was going on.

Of course, the dirt around the old ditch and by the window was undisturbed. Beto was sitting there when all of a sudden, he heard the sound again (a shovel going into the dirt). Beto looked around but saw nothing, again he heard the sound and this time he noticed a piece of cardboard which was lodged into the adobe with a piece sticking out and every time there was a small breeze the cardboard would scratch against the adobe, making the sound. Needless to say, Beto tore off that piece of cardboard and never heard that sound again.

I cracked up laughing and told Beto, his wife Martha and my wife Gloria who were with us of how I had had the same experience when I had slept in that same room one night while I was sick. This was the first time I had ever told anyone of my experience that night when I was sick. Beto laughed and said that neither had he, he had forgotten about it till now.

So, we solved what was making the noise, but why did we both of us see the same old man?

STORY 3

THE MONKEY

This story was told to me by my grandmother Natalia. It took place in a small mining town called Fresnillo in Zacatecas Mexico in the late 1890's. My grandmother had a brother who lived in Fresnillo, and she would frequently visit and stay in Fresnillo for days. She didn't tell me, and I didn't ask if she or her brother knew this man personally (who the story is about), but the story goes like this.

There was this man who lived by himself in a one room adobe house on top of a small hill. And there were no neighbors for some distance around. The man was a miner and worked in some local mines. Since the mines were some distance away, the man had to walk to work every day. The man would leave his house early in the morning and would return late in the evening. After a long day at work the man would arrive home hungry and tired. He often wondered if it wouldn't be better if he had someone at home to prepare his dinner when he got home. But that was just wishful thinking as he realized it could not be. Sometimes he was so tired he went to sleep without dinner but not without praying.

It was unknown if the man had a wife or children somewhere else. As it was not unusual for some man to come to work by themselves while their families lived somewhere else. Either way, if he did, they were not with him at the time.

One day when the man arrived home from work, he found a chimpanzee sitting down by his front and only door to his house. The man looked at the chimpanzee who seemed very friendly and asked him" now where did you come from?" The man looked around hoping to see someone in the area to no avail. "Ha" the man says opening the door to his house. As the man opened the door the chimpanzee walked right in behind him. "I wonder if you didn't escape from some nearby circus "the man told the chimpanzee. This was the only thought that came to the man at the time as it was unusual for this type of animal to be lose in the area as no such animals lived there, you would only see them when the circus came around.

The chimpanzee would reach up and hold the man's hand as if wanting for the man to grab it and lead the chimpanzee around. "Are you hungry?" the man asked the chimpanzee who seemed to understand everything the man was saying. The chimpanzee right away made himself at home. "Let me fix us something to eat" he tells the chimpanzee as he walked up to the kitchen area of the room.

The one room house was composed with one side of the room being were the man had his bed and dresser. On the center wall was a fireplace which also served as the area for cooking. Some piled wood was next to it. And on the opposite side wall from where his bed was, the man had some planks of wood attached to the wall serving as shelves where he had cooking utensils and such. A small table with two chairs was in the middle of the room.

After preparing something to eat the man served the chimpanzee on a plate and noticed that the chimpanzee knew how to use a fork and a knife. "Well," said the man; "you are definably well educated and trained, and you have good manners, you much be a very valuable little monkey." They ate and afterwards the man cleaned the dishes and pans while the little chimpanzee sat looking at him.

"Tomorrow I am going to ask around to see who might have lost you" he tells the chimpanzee. "I bet there is someone who is looking for you and who is missing you very much, as you are very well trained and must belong to someone important."

That evening as it was getting late, and the man was preparing to go to bed the chimpanzee started to dance around and entertain the man with its dances and jumping around. The man laughed and enjoyed what the chimpanzee was doing but finally told the chimpanzee that they would have to go to sleep. The man pulled out some extra blankets and laid them on the floor apposite to the wall where he had his bed. The chimpanzee rolled up into a ball with his back towards the man and went to sleep while the man prayed his rosary in silence. The man had a devotion to the Blessed Virgin and prayed his rosary every night.

The next day the man gets up and see's that the cheerful chimpanzee is already up and after a quick breakfast and after he made his lunch the man goes to work and decides to close the door and not risk the chance that the chimpanzee might walk away and get lost. The man figured he would ask around and for sure someone will have left word that they were missing the little monkey.

Nobody around the mines knew anything about a missing chimpanzee. That evening when he got home, he found the chimpanzee still in the house and the house had been cleaned and supper was already prepared. "Wow" says the man" don't tell me you prepared dinner by yourself?" "And look "says the man" you even cleaned the house; you definitely are a very well trained and educated little monkey"

The chimpanzee seemed to be happy and jumped up on the man's arms. The man played with the chimpanzee for a few minutes then they had dinner. That night seemed a repeat of the previous night.

In the morning when the man woke up and started to get ready for work, he noticed the chimpanzee was up and had already prepared the man's lunch and had breakfast ready. "Muchas gracias" the man tells the chimpanzee. The man ate breakfast and kept praising the monkey for its intelligence. After a quick breakfast the man tells the chimpanzee," We will see you tonight" and he pats the chimpanzee on his way out the door, still amazed with the monkey.

This same scenario was repeated for the next couple of days until the weekend came. On Sunday the man was off from work, and he would always go to church. The man figured this would be a perfect opportunity to take the chimpanzee with him to church and see if he could find the monkey's owner.

However, the man could not get the chimpanzee up to take him to church and even wondered if the little monkey had not gotten sick. The man finally decided to go to church without the chimpanzee.

After church services the man went up to the priest and told him about the monkey that he had in his house. The man explained to the priest of how intelligent the monkey was and of the many things that it could do. Oh, said the priest, I hope it's not something bad. Oh, no the man said, it's nothing bad; it's a good little monkey which had been very well trained. The priest assured the man that he would ask around to see if anyone knew anything a missing monkey. The priest also said that regardless of the findings he would pay him a visit on Tuesday. The man agreed and left.

When the man got home the chimpanzee was up as if nothing had happened and had dinner waiting.

On Tuesday when the man got home from work the chimpanzee as usual had dinner ready. This time the man held off from eating for a while as he was waiting for the priest to arrive, and he wanted to surprise the priest with the dinner. A short while later there was a knock on the door. As the man opened the door the priest stepped in spraying holy water into the house and saying prayers in Latin. Upon seeing this, the monkey let out a big scream, ran towards the wall jumping and smashing itself into the wall as if trying to get out. The priest continued throwing holy water on the spot that the monkey had left on the wall. The man just stood there amazed as if in shock not saying a word just looking at the priest as he continued to spray holy water on the spot. The black spot seemed to shrink until it was about the size of an apple. The man just stood there with his mouth wide open staring at the spot on the wall wondering what had happened.

The priest then started to interrogate the man as to everything that had occurred in the house since the chimpanzee had arrived. Upon further questioning the man then remembered and realized that every evening when he was getting ready to pray the rosary the monkey always seemed to try and distract the man from praying by dancing around and playing and when he insisted the monkey would lay down with his face towards the wall and back towards the man.

The priest figured that since the man had a great devotion to the Blessed Virgin Mary and had made a promise many years ago to pray the rosary every night no matter what that the monkey was something evil and that if for any reason, he had not prayed his rosary as promised that the monkey who was actual a devil, would have taken his soul.

STORY 4

THE ROCK MAN

When I was about six years old my grandmother took me to see the church of El Santo Niño de Atocha in Plateros close to Fresnillo (where her brother lived) Mexico. It was my first time traveling into Mexico and my first time on a train. It was an adventure and although I can't remember much, I do recall the train stops where ladies came around with food baskets on their heads selling Mexican sandwiches and sweet bread.

The reason grandma was taking me was because, as I understand it, I almost choked on a piece of baloney (I still love it) when I was an infant. My grandmother being a devotee of El Santo Niño de Atocha at the moment while I was having trouble breathing promised to El Niño that she would take me to see him should he saved my life, which he did.

During the long trip My grandmother told me a story which I still haven't forgotten and which I will relay to you. But to better understand who El Santo Niño de Atocha is and why there was so much devotion to him in those days, I think its best that I explain the history behind El Niño de Atocha.

El Santo Niño de Atocha is portrayed as a small Spanish pilgrim boy, the image of the child Jesus known as Santo Niño de Atocha is dressed in a long gown with a cape that has a wide lace collar and frilled cuffs. The traditional symbol of a pilgrim, a cockleshell, is

11

on his cape, and he holds a little basket in his left hand and a water gourd suspended from a staff in his right hand. The little holy boy wears buckled sandals –huaraches- of silver, and a large, floppy hat with a feather. Although he is known as a wanderer, he is usually shown seated in a little chair. Depending on the part of the Country the dress attire may vary a little.

In those days in Atocha, a suburb of Madrid, many men were imprisoned because of their faith. The prisoners were not fed by their jailors, so food was taken to them by their families. At one time the caliph issued an order that no one except children twelve years old and younger would be permitted to bring food to the prisoners. Those with young children would manage to keep their relatives alive, but what of the others?

The women of the town appealed to Our Lady, begging her to help them find a way to feed their husbands, sons, and brothers. Soon the children came home from the prison with a strange story. Those prisoners who had no young children to feed them were being visited and fed by a young boy. None of the children knew who he was, but the little water gourd he carried was never empty, and there was always plenty of bread in his basket to feed all the helpless prisoners who were without children of their own to bring them their food. Apparently, he came at night, slipping past the sleeping guards or smiling politely at those who were alert, and he was never challenged.

Those who had asked the Virgin of Atocha for a miracle began to suspect the identity of the little boy. Later using the description given by the young children a figure and Legend were born.

However, years later as if in confirmation, it was noticed that the shoes on the statue of the child Jesus were worn down. When they replaced the shoes with new ones, those too were worn out.

After Ferdinand and Isabella drove the Moors from Spain in 1492, the people continued to invoke the aid of Our Lady of the Atocha and her Holy Child.

When the Spaniards came to the New World, they brought along the devotions of their native regions. Those from Madrid naturally brought their devotion to Our Lady of the Atocha. In 1540, silver mines were found in Mexico, and Spanish mineworkers migrated here.

In Plateros, a tiny village near the mines of Fresnillo, a church was built in honor of Santo Cristo de los Plateros, a miraculous crucifix, beginning in the late 1690s. A beautiful Spanish image of Our Lady and her Divine child was placed on a side altar. Being that my grandmother was born and raised only a few hours away in Aguascalientes, she as well as many other people from around the area had great faith on the Niño.

Now, the story my grandmother told me goes like this. Some years back a man from Guanajuato had been in need of a miracle and had asked El Niño to do the favor of granting his wish. If granted, he would walk all the way from Guanajuato to Plateros to personally thank him for the favor granted. As it goes the favor was indeed granted and one day the man started out on his journey to repay the debt. Some distance away the man started to have second thoughts as the hours turned into days and he was getting tired. Still some distance away from Plateros, he sat down on a rock regretting he had made the promise and thought to himself" forget it; it's too hard I am not going any further, I should have never promised this stupid promise". At that moment the man turned into stone, a big rock looking like a man sitting down.

For years many people who passed by that road on their way, in the direction of Plateros and coming across the rock and knowing the story would push the rock and cause it to roll towards Plateros. People who knew the story were helping the now rock man to complete his journey. Each time someone pushed the rock it roll closer to Platero's. According to grandma the man was getting closer to his destination each year.

I never went back to Mexico until 1994 and between 1994 and 2008 due to my work in Mexico I went various times to and around the area of Zacatecas. As I was working in Mexico at the time and the whole area was part of my work area. I often passed by Plateros and Fresnillo and often stayed in the city of Zacatecas which was not too far from Plateros. Whenever I could, my wife and I would stop at the old church and visit. I could never get enough of the old church nor the small village where it was located at ; it was fascinating just to be there. My wife would accompany me often and she too was intrigued with the place. I also tried looking for relatives but always being short of time never had enough time to properly check. Most were living in Aguascalientes.

People who have had miracles granted and who have gone to visit and repay their granted wish at the church often leave behind things like letters, silver tokens, flowers, and all kinds of appreciation trinkets. There are so many, that a large room has been built next to the church to accommodate the many crutches, wheelchairs, and other sizable items. People keep leaving things even now, year after year after more miracles are granted.

Whenever possible I would ask the attendants who sell souvenirs and maintain the area if they had heard the story of the rock man. Although many people had heard of the story no one knew what ever happened to the rock man or where it was located. Some people said that the old road did not exist anymore, and that the statue had long been lost. So, I have no way of knowing if that man ever made it to Plateros, and if he did, what happened to him.

STORY 5

THE THING IN THE DESERT

This story was told to us by my father Demecio. It was repeated various times as I grew up. It happened during the early 1950's while he was clearing out some desert land for a new farm that was being built in Dell City Texas. Not only did it involved clearing the land but also establishing an irrigation system, it was all being done from scratch. Dell City was a new community and other farms had either just been established or were in the process.

Common planting in the area was alfalfa, cotton, and other various crops. Dad's work entailed working long hours and nighttime as well. It included night watering the newly planted cotton and other crops and he always had Spotty our dog with him as a companion as he was very often by himself. During the early commencement of the farm, it was only my dad and the owner Bob Travis.

There was nothing around the new farm but desert and a few hundred acres of cleared and newly planted grounds. Our house which was the closest building was about three miles way. I don't know how much acreage the ranch was composed of, but it was Hugh.

Dad told us that one morning around 3:00 o'clock he was watering and rechanneling water on some newly planted rolls. Dad said that he had gotten his rubber boots muddy and had stopped to clean them with the shovel when he heard Spotty growl. Spotty was looking towards an area not yet cleared for planting and which had a bunch of small humps of dirt with mesquite bushes growing on them. The area was pitch- dark and there was hardly any moon light that night. Dad pointed his Lateran towards Spotty and the dark area and he could see the hairs on spotty's back standing up as he barked towards the dark area. That only meant one thing to dad, and he asked Spotty "what is it boy" thinking all the time that it was probably a coyote or some other type of animal.

There were many animals in the still savage area, and they would usually come out at night to eat. But it was uncommon for Spotty to bark at them as he was this time and in the manner in which he was doing it. To a certain extant he had kind of gotten use to many of the regular animals and would bark differently. Especially if Spotty felt no threat. These animals were usually coyotes and jack rabbits and unless Spotty felt threatened, he wouldn't bark at all. This time Spotty's bark was not a "hey, guys what are you doing?" type of bark. This time it was like a "hey, what the...... who are you?" type of bark. As Spotty sounded with a low whimpering sound, Dad knew it was an "I am getting afraid" type of sound. Dad became concerned as he saw how Spotty was staring, focusing motionless in the dark.

Dad then walked a short distance to where the tractor was at which was still running and maneuvered it to so that the tractor lights pointed towards the direction spotty was growling. Since the tractors lights did not shine to far, Dad decided to move the tractor slowly towards the direction Spotty was indicating and while doing so Spotty started to bark really loud and started backing up at the same time. At about forty yards away Dad saw something move really quick behind some mesquite bushes. The object looked like a large white sheet. It looked like when the wind catches a large rag and blows it away only to be caught by and struck in another mesquite bush. But this time it was fast and seemed precise as if intentionally stopping behind the bush.

It was hard to see clearly as the tractor lights were dim at that distance, Dad could barely see a white shadowy outline behind the large bush. Spotty kept barking and running back and forth for about 20 yards towards and away from the object. Spotty suddenly stopped dead on its tracks as the white object moved real fast again from one of the mesquite bushes it was behind and moved towards a bush which was closer in their direction. Whatever it was, it was not afraid of them, as it had moved towards them knowing they were there. Any other known animal would at this time run away in fear of the dog, and tractor lights. There was no wind at all, so whatever it was it was, it was moving under its own power. Spotty then started to back track slowly and started to make a whining sound again.

Dad had never seen Spotty back down from man or beast before. Dad started to get nervous at this time and got his rifle that he always carried with him by the tractors seat. Dad fired a few shots at the object with his .22 as he stood on top of the tractor. Dad wanted to scare off whatever it was. The object did not move at all. The object looked to be about the size of a cow or something like that and it was able to move really fast. This time Dad carefully aimed at the object and fired. But again, the object did not move. Again, he fired but the object just seemed to have slowly moved over to another mesquite further away.

It was at this time that Dad called Spotty back and got him in the tractor with him. Dad then decided to drive fast forward towards the object with the tractor with the rifle in one hand and driving with the other using the tractor as a shield. Whatever it was, dad was ready to confront it. However due to the many mesquite mounts Dad had to constantly be turning the steering wheel to go around them causing him not to be able to drive to fast nor in a straight line and would on occasions lose sight of where the object was. When finally, they got to the area where he thought they had last seen the object, nothing could be found. By this time Spotty was no longer barking. Spotty was standing up with its hands on the tractors seat, its ears standing up and focusing ahead. Dad got off the tractor and with the help of the lantern looked all around for some type of prints on the ground but was unable to find anything. The only prints to be seen where Dad's and Spotty's,

Dad said that for a while be got a little scared and mainly because of the way Spotty was acting. Spotty seemed to fear whatever it was that was out there and Spotty never feared anything.

It was never known what it might have been that dad and spotty saw that night. But whatever it was, they were glad they never saw it again.

STORY 6

THE DANCE

This story was told to me by my mom when I was around 13 years old. It took place in a neighborhood called San Juan which is located on the central east part of El Paso Texas. San Juan is close to Val Verde where we kids were born and raised. It's in a northeasterly direction. The area had a reputation for being wild and rough even in my days.

This incident took place in the mid 1930's. The area just like Val Verde was prominently Hispanic with most of the people who settled in the area having come from Mexico just like our Val Verde neighborhood and included the same language, and customs.

As I mentioned before the neighborhood had gained a pretty bad reputation during those days which lasted to the mid 1960's. It was known for liquor trafficking during prohibition, gangs, and drug trafficking among other things.

The story goes that on one summer evening a girl who lived in San Juan had asked her mother for permission to attend a local dance. Every weekend there were dances in a local dance hall. This dance hall didn't have a very good reputation and the mother refused to allow her daughter to attend this particular dance the particular Saturday night. The mother felt her daughter was too young and had no business in a place like that. Especially since she was going by herself and not having a chaperon. The mother tried to reason with her daughter and gave the girl several reasons why she couldn't go but the girl was not satisfied with any of them. The girl threw a fit and said she was going to go anyway with or without her permission. The mother pleaded with the girl, but she would only scream and yell at her mother and said she was going no matter what. Later that night the girl slipped out of the house without her mother knowing and went to the dance.

The girl knew most of the people at the dance, since most were from the neighborhood. But it wasn't unusual for people from the surrounding area to attend these dances as well. However, this girl didn't really seem to care to associate much with the other girls and seemed to stay more to herself. One reason was that the attendees at the dance for the most part were much other than her. The girl seemed more interested in flirting with boys, dancing and getting their attention.

It wasn't long before a handsome well-dressed young gentleman walked into the dance hall. He appeared a little older than the usual crowd. Everyone eyed this person out as he was dressed way beyond what the local boys could ever afford and seemed out of place. To make things worse he was very handsome, and all the girls were competing for his attention and hoping that he would notice them. This young man walked around for a while acting confident and sure of himself eyeing things out.

Usually when a stranger such as this walked into the dance hall and the local boys didn't him, he would quickly be challenge and even thrown out of the dance hall and /or beaten up. The local boys didn't take much for strangers in their barrio. Even more when the stranger acted in such a way.

The locals felt as if the stranger was moving in on their turf without their approval. But in this case, for some unknown reason it seemed as if the local boys were either afraid or at least hesitant to act, or just simply in such an astonishment that they froze.

The girls too seemed to be in trance. They could not believe what they were seeing. Everyone was just staring at him unable to digest what was happening.

The stranger walked up to the girl who had sneaked out of her house that night and asked her to dance. The girl quickly accepted feeling special, proud, and acted as if she was the envy of all the other girls. After all it had been her who the stranger had chosen. The girl and the stranger danced and were seen laughing and enjoying themselves throughout the night.

Both of them were also consuming alcoholic beverages which although not unusually, it was unusual for anyone to be going it out in the open. To begin with the girls who attended the dance usually did not drink. Most of the time it would be the boys who drank, and they would sneak outside and do their consuming out of sight. The main reason for this was that alcohol was prohibited at the time plus the fact that many were under aged.

Late that night people reported seeing both the stranger and the girl walk outside of the dance hall together, as if they were leaving. Ten or fifteen minutes later the music was interrupted a very loud chilling, hair raising screams coming from the outside. So loud that it overpowered the music. Without thinking everyone ran to see what was going on and after a short search in the dark someone yelled that there was a girl in inside of an irrigation ditch that ran next to the dance hall. The girl was found lying face up with her eyes wide open, scratches all about the face and her throat was cut. The girl was obviously dead.

The police were called, and an investigation was conducted. It was quickly determined that the stranger had done the deed. But no one knew the stranger that had come into the dance that night. No one saw him arrive, so they didn't know what type of transportation he was using. For sure he was not a local resident. Most could only describe the stranger as very handsome and debonair. Some did say that the stranger seemed to limp from one leg as if he had an injured foot. The scratches found on the girl were described as the type of scratches that a roaster or cat could have made. And the police said that the cuts around the neck seemed to have been done by something other than a regular knife. Also, bites were found on the girl's shoulders which were deep in nature similar to animal type bite marks.

Later on, rumors surfaced in the neighborhood and people were saying that the stranger was actual the devil. There was also the rumor that some people had actually seen that the stranger's left foot and that it was that of a goat.

The case was never solved, and the stranger was never again seen around the area. The dance hall was eventually closed due to other mishaps.

STORY 7

THE MIDGET

I was about five or six years old when the following story took place. I can remember only certain things of what went on that day, and it would take my mom to fill in the blanks some years later. My younger sister's Angie and Yolanda and older sister Guadalupe were also with me when this happened.

Every year the whole family would make a trip to visit our uncles in Ojinaga Mexico(my father's two brothers). This was done usually during the summer months. We lived in El Paso at the time and mom and dad would put my sisters and me into the family sedan and away we would go. Our brother Gilbert would sometimes accompany us.

The trip would take about six hours to get to Presidio Texas. From Presidio we would drive over a bridge and cross into Ojinaga Mexico. From Ojinaga it took some more time to get where my uncles lived through dirt roads which were meant more for horses and horse carriages then automobiles.

But first my dad would stop at the local radio station so that they could make an announcement that we were there. There were no phones or other type of communications at the time to the small farming community where my uncles lived so, the radio was a the best and only means of communicating. If my uncles didn't hear the message,usually some neighbor would, and they would relay the message.

On one of those regular trips occurred during a sizzling summer day in the mid 1950's after visiting and on our way back to El Paso we had an incident. We had already left Presidio and were in the U.S. and left Mexico behind some miles away and were in a long stretch of barren highway when our car over heated. My dad checked the engine and found that a radiator hose had sprung a leak and to make things worse we had no water. We were about ten miles past Shafter an old mining town and thirty miles from Presidio and about forty miles from Marfa Texas. And although this was the main road between Marfa and Presidio there was not a car in sight.

The only good thing was that it was daylight. We had no choice but to wait (no cell phones in those days) for a car to pass by to give us some help. We waited to what seemed like forever for us kids and after a while we became hungry and thirsty and as it usually happens when you have young kids, we started complaining that we were hungry and thirsty and some of us were crying.

It must have been around noon time and the heat was unbearable. It was so unbearable that I remember my sisters crying. (By the way very few cars had air conditioners in those days) Dad became impatient after hearing us cry and no cars going by and told my mom that he was going walk to Shafter which was closer and see if he could find some help. Maybe he could catch a ride along the way. Mom felt it was a bad idea and suggested that it was better for them to wait. Mom said somebody had to drive by soon and she started to pray to *el Niño de Atocha* for help (see story 4). El Nino de Atocha was someone my mom and grandmother were always praying to for help when ever there was a crisis (I must make a clarification here, we Catholics don't pray or worship Saints, we ask them for their intervention with our Lord since they were able to accomplish such height and are close to him. We ask them to take our prayers like a bouquet of flowers to our Lord and ask him to grant us our plea).

Mom closed her eyes as she prayed while dad stood outside the car with the car hood open waiting to see if someone would pass by.

No more than about ten minutes had gone by when dad yelled out that someone was coming. A large flatbed truck was coming from the direction of Shafter. The truck then pulled up next to our car and I could see about half a dozen fifty-gallon barrels on the back of the truck which were so full that they were spilling water from the overflow as the truck stopped.

After the truck pulled up the driver jumped out from the truck. The driver was a young Anglo cowboy and was wearing the whole cowboy attire, a cowboy hat, spares, and boots and even had chaps. The shocking surprise to everyone was that he was a midget. I recall staring at him because I had never seen such a small man like this before. You couldn't tell he was a midget while he was driving. It was not until he jumped out of the truck that one could see how small he really was. I recall my sisters were also astonished upon seeing the midget. The midget then walked up to my dad and asked him if he needed any help. Dad explained our situation as the midget kept looking towards the inside of the car. Mom then asked if we could have some water and the midget said that that was not a problem that he had plenty of water in the barrels.

In no time the midget jumped up on the bed of his truck and handed dad a couple of pales of water for us kids and the car. The cowboy had some black tape and he helped dad patch up the water hose. While working on the car dad and the midget conversed and dad thanked him for stopping to help us. The midget said that it was no problem that he went by here all the time. Dad asked if he was from the area and the midget said yes that he was from a ranch close by.

Once the temporary repair had been done dad started the car and the cowboy told dad to drive ahead, that he would follow us up to Marfa to make sure we got there okay. It took us maybe half an hour to get to Marfa. As we neared Marfa and were about to pull in into a service station, dad looked back to see if the midget was also pulling into the service station behind us. Mom and Dad had been talking and Mom had suggested that they should give him some money as a gratitude for stopping and helping us out. But when dad looked back in his rear-view mirror, he could no longer see the midget's truck. Dad told mom this and they both wondered where the midget had gone. Dad said that he had just seen him through the rear-view mirror a couple of minutes ago. Dad said that maybe the midget felt they were safe and had turned off somewhere.

In Marfa dad pulled into a small garage and filling station to have the car checked and buy some bread and baloney for us. While having the water hose replaced dad told the mechanic of what had happened and of the midget in the truck that had helped us. The mechanic swore that he knew every farmer and rancher in the whole area and that there were no midgets in the area. Dad kept telling the mechanic that he was sure and described the midget and the truck to the mechanic. But again, the mechanic said he knew everyone from Presidio all the way to Valentine and there was no one like that. Dad again described the truck and again the mechanic just smiled and said nope, no truck like that around here.

Dad didn't tell us about this conversation until later when he had gotten the car fixed and we were on the road again and actually, he was conversing between mom and not us kids. I remember mom and dad talking about it as we drove and mom saying *"bendito sea dios, era el Santo Niño de Atocha." (Bless be God, it was the Santo Nino de Atocha).*

One good thing happened as result of this, from that time on Dad would never make a trip without carrying a canvas water pouch with water that he would hang on the front of the truck or car.

And as for the midget? Well? who knows!

STORY 8

THE LOCKED DOOR

This story comes from my father-in-law Alejandro Renova. It took place when he was a teenager in the 1930's and growing up in a Hacienda known as Capilla de los Remedios in the Mexican State of Chihuahua. This small farming community was composed mainly of family who were related either by birth or marriage. These families were descendants of the original settlers of the area in the mid to late 1800's and included up to 4 generations. There were about a dozen houses and the streets were dirt and of course there was no electricity. Kerosene lanterns were used to light the houses. There was also no plumping or running water. A common well supplied the water plus a small river and a lake that was close by. The closes town of any significance was Cuauhtémoc.

Outside of the daily chores with the farming, ranching and household chores was the caring for various animals such as chickens, pigs, and horses and cows. As for entertainment, there was not much except for an occasional competition of roping and racing. There was not much to do around the area for teenagers and besides there was usually no free time as chores took up all the time. When crops where not being harvest or planted it was an all-hands-on board and it was almost a 7-24 operation. If time permitted kids would usually gather at night and talk.

Since there were no streetlights, the area would be dark and if one was to venture outside for any distance, lanterns were used to light the way.

My father-in-law lived with his mother, father, and older brother (who usually wasn't home) in a two-room adobe house. There was only one door for the entrance to the house which lead to the kitchen area. The other attached room was the bedroom area where they all slept. The floors were dirt floors. All the houses were a short walk distance from each other only separated by horse and cow corrals and some barns and maybe a small vegetable garden.

One evening my father-in-law had asked permission to go out with the area kids and he was told not to stay up late and to be home early. However, kids being kids and the conversations being very interesting, my father-in-law stayed later than he should have. When he realized how late it was, he ran home. Being that everyone knew everyone there was no need for locks on the doors and people for the most part left doors unlocked if they had a lock at all. At my in-laws house the door could only be locked from the inside which was for privacy.

When my father-in-law got home, he found the door locked from the inside. Which meant someone was home. Realizing that he was late and that he had made his mother angry he knew some punishment was due. He knocked and got no answer. He continued knocking and calling out to his mother to open the door. He asked his mother to please let him in, that he was sorry he was late. But still no reply. He felt his mother was really angry this time as he had now been knocking for some time and was wondering what he was going to do. As it was it didn't take much for his mother to become angry and he felt he was being punished by not allowing him to enter.

After a few more times of trying to convince his mother to open the door with no results, my father-in-law sat down by the door figuring eventually the door would have to open. My father-in-law could hear someone throwing water on the floor inside the house as it was customary after washing the dishes the women would throw the water on the dirt floor which would also help to keep the dust under control. Upon hearing that water being thrown on the floor, again my father-in-law started to plea with his mother to let him in. He just sat down again and decided to wait until his mother got over it and opened the door. He thought, for sure she's not going to let me stay here all night.

As he sat there on the door's step, he suddenly saw at a distance some people walking and talking on the street coming towards his house using a lantern for light. As they got nearer, he realized it was his mother and father. When they got there, he asked them who was inside the house. At this time my father-in-law thought his brother was inside and had been messing with him. His parents said, no one is in the house as they walked pass him and pushed the door open. To his surprise the door had been unlocked all the time, but he was sure it was locked cause he tried various times to open it. He told his parents of what had happened, and they just simply laughed at him. He kept repeating of what he had heard and how the door was locked from the inside. His mother simply said he was crazy. Nobody believed him, but he swore on what he heard and that he tried opening the door and it was locked.

STORY 9

THE HEADLESS CHARRO

This next story also happened to my father-in-law in the Hacienda where he was raised called the "La Capilla." (See story 8) When this happened my father-in-law was older and already married.

Whenever you traveled on the dirt roads of La Capilla you constantly have to be stopping to open and close cattle gates. In many cases it's because of the different owned partial of land that are fenced in, and each has its own gate to keep cattle and other livestock from wondering off. Even when its areas owned by the same person, they often separate areas for grazing cattle, horses, and areas that were used for planting and sometimes the grazing areas are rotated, and this would keep the grazing animals from wondering into agricultural areas and eating up the plants. These gates are normally made of wire and tree limbs (or other lumber or wood) and are as wide as the dirt road and four to five feet high. Bale wires are used for hinges and a looped with the wire is made on the opposite side and used to put over the top end of the fence post to lock the gate into place and keep it from swinging open.

Having experienced traveling through this area I have to say it's a pain in the bud having to get off of the truck, open the gate, wait for the truck to pass then closing the gate again and this is over and over again.

One day my father-in-law says that Raul (a relative) asked him if he would accompany him to deliver a truck load of wheat to Cuauhtémoc. My father-in-law agreed with the condition that on the way back they would stop and buy some feed for his horses. Due to the constant bad dirt roads (especially after rain) which causes a vehicle to have to go slow avoiding holes and making regular curves and avoiding wash offs along the road it can make the thirty-five miles to Cuauhtémoc take a couple of hours. Also, not to mention the many times that one has to stop and open and close gates along the way.

Raul and my father-in-law started off early one day with the loaded truck and by noon where in Cuauhtémoc. By the time they unloaded and picked up the feed for the horses and had gotten lunch it had become late. On their way back as customary, Raul would stop the truck just before a gate and my father-in-law would get out of the truck and run over to open the gate for the truck to go through. Once Raul's truck cleared the gate Raul would stop and wait for my father-in-law while he closed the gate and got back in the truck.

Just before getting into the La Capilla's property there is one last gate and by the time they got there it was already dark, and they had to rely on the trucks headlights to see. However, the familiarity with the area helped a lot. Raul stopped in front of the last gate, my father-in-law ran over and opened the gate and Raul drove by. As my father-in-law was about to close the gate, he saw with the help of the truck lights reflection what seemed like a big yellowish cow moving as if wanting to go through the gate. Due to the darkness certain details could not be seen clear. My father-in-law figured he better open the gate wider (he had already started to close it) to allow the cow to go through. As he stepped aside to allow the cow more clearance the cow was now observed to be a big yellowish horse and the saddle was eye level to my father-in-law. My father-in-law looked up and observed a rider on the horse who was wearing an old type of Charro custom with shinning silver spurs and shiny buttons running down the side of the pants.

As the horse and rider went by my father-in-law again looked up at the man in a Charro custom and he noticed that the man was headless, or at least my father-in-law could not see a head. As soon as the horse cleared the gate my father-in-law ran to the truck and jumped in all excited and looking back and asking Raul at the same time if he had seen the headless Charro. Raul who was in the truck with his back towards the gate all the time, said he saw nothing.

My father-in-law would later say that he was so scared that he didn't remember if he closed the gate or not. Later on, in the La Capilla my father-in-law would repeat his story and he was amazed to find out that other people had also seen this same headless Charro at other times. Some of the elders said that the same Charro had been appearing in the area for many years and that it was believed to be the original owner of the La Capilla. People who had lived there years ago and who had known the owner of the properties had said that the original owner always dressed in that fashion and had a big buck skin mare which at times looked yellowish.

But why headless? No one knew or would say.

STORY 10

THE HORSE FACE

This story came from my grandmother. It is something that happened to my grandfather when he was still a young unmarried man.

I was seven years old when my grandfather died and although I don't remember him much, I do recall him as a white-haired old man, and he was already ill, and I didn't have much interaction with him. I mostly remember him being in bed and sometimes hearing him saying nonsense stuff. Mom and Grandma would sometimes have me sit by his bed and keep an eye on him and make sure he didn't get up. That was because he had the tendency to want to get up and more than once when he fell. My job was to yell at mom and grandma and let them know if he was trying to get up.

I do remember that my grandpa only had one eye having lost one to an accident and we wore a fake glass eye. They would keep his fake eye in a water glass next to his bed. I remember staring close up to the water glass and looking at the eye, which was looking back at me, it was weird.

One time he asked me who that man standing by his bed was (there was no one there) and he would talk to the man asking him in Spanish "who are you, what do you want." It freak me out as he would talk to people that were not there.

Later on, after grandpa died, and I was older grandma would tell me all kinds of stories of grandpa as he participated in the Mexican revolution and even went to jail one time, and he was going to be executed for treason but was able to escape with the help of his cousin. Grandma told me many stories and one that stuck with me went like this.

As a young man and during the revolution my grandfather worked for the Mexican railroad. On one occasion they were in a small village close to Guadalajara Jalisco. According to my grandmother he started working for the Mexican Railroad while still a teenager and was able to advance through the ranks to becoming a group leader.

On this particular day they were working close to this village where many of the men would frequently visit after work. The men either lived inside rail cars or tents and on the evening needed some place to rest and enjoy themselves. One of the favorites places to visit in this village was a local watering hole where the workers would have a refreshments (liquor), play pool, listen to music, and relax after a hard day's work.

My grandmother said that in those days my grandfather was a boozer and although not necessarily a troublemaker, he would never walk away from what he called a "fun time" even if it involved a god drunken brawl.

My grandfather had a close friend with whom he would always hangout with and with whom he would always seem to get involved in mischief. These two young men were inseparable.

This evening after my grandfather and his friend had been drinking for most of the evening, they found themselves drunk and out of money, so they decided to leave the bar. It was close to sun set when they started down the main dirt street. Small adobe homes were situated alongside the dusty road and as they walked, they noticed a young senorita sitting outside in front of a house combing her long black hair. It was customary in those days, especially in scorching summer days, for ladies to sit outside their homes and brush dry their hair after a bath or after washing their hair. For the most part woman wore their hair long in those days and it took a lot of combing to take out all the knots and dry the hair. The cool breeze would also help with the drying.

As they passed by the senorita my grandfather's friend stopped to flirt with the young lady who instantly turned her back towards him. My grandfather's friend kept on talking to the lady, asking her for her name and telling her how sweet she smelled and so on. Each time he tried to get close to try and take a look at her face she could turn and lower her face so that my grandfather's friend would not see her. All the time my grandfather just stood there not wanting to interfere and allowing his friend the opportunity to meet the young lady. My grandfather's friend kept on telling the girl "Come on sweetheart show me your pretty face."

After a while the girl stood up and starting walking away towards the end of the street walking in a manner to where her face was still not visible. There were only about a dozen houses and the bar on this particular street. The man continued behind the girl, still making sweet comments at her and my grandfather followed behind. At the end of the street the girls started walking towards some open fields which had been recently plowed and she walked between the rolls. My grandfather figured it was time to give up on this girl as it was obvious, she was playing too hard to get and told his friend to give it up. "NO" said his friend, this girl knows us and that's why she is playing hard to get. I'm going to follow her, and I am going to find out who she is, if I have to walk all the way to hell, my grandfather's friend said.

At this time my grandfather said "Well, you go ahead. I am tired and I'll wait for you here." At this my grandfather walked underneath a tree that had some large logs on the ground and sat on one of them to wait.

My grandfather watched as the lady and his friend kept walking away, each time his friend getting close to her and trying to sneak a peek at her face only to have the lady turn towards the other side and cover her face with her hair. Finally, they were both out of sight and my grandfather just sat there.

It was getting late, and the sun was already half down when my grandfather saw his friend running back towards his direction. The way the man was running was somewhat unusual. My grandfather stood up to meet him and saw that his friend had a very scary face with his eyes and mouth wide open as if in shock. The friend didn't even seem to have noticed my grandfather standing there and was about to go pass my grandfather when my grandfather stood in his way and stopped him by holding on to his shoulders. My grandfather kept asking him what was wrong and what happened, and the friend was just started at my grandfather and started to point back towards from where he had just come from and mumbling "Aye, aye, aye" and the man fainted and fell to the ground.

Grandfather tried to bring him back talking to him and gently slapping the man on the face, but nothing worked. My grandfathers than ran to the bar and got some help to take the man to a clinic close to the railroad station.

His friend was in a comma type condition for some days. When he finally came out of the coma and for a long time, he wouldn't talk to anyone of what had happened. However, months later he confided in grandfather and told him the following.

He said that he had continued after the girl for some distance and that finally the girl stopped abruptly and said" you want to see my face? Okay, look at me" and the girl turned around. To his amazement and surprise the girl had the face of a horse with a long nose, big red eyes and fire coming out of the nostros. My grandfather's friend could only recall being so frighten that he panicked and for a while could not move. He couldn't remember running away or anything else. He couldn't remember what he did after seeing the face. He could only recall waking up at the clinic. He did recall praying to the Virgin Mary out loud and that's all.

Needless to say, my grandfather's friend never drank again and became a different man. He changed so much that he no longer spent time together with my grandfather, or should I say, my grandfather never hanged around with him.

My grandfather continued with his old ways and didn't change, he simply said that his friend had been so drunk that he thought he had seen what he saw. But something happened, and it was dramatic enough to be able to change that man grandma would say.

STORY 11

THE SCREAMING COFFIN

During the early 1900 Mexico was going through a huge influenza epidemic which was killing off thousands of its people. (Not only in Mexico but throughout the world) The epidemic was all over and affected all of Mexico and no city or village was exempt. In fact, both of my father's parents perished in that epidemic leaving my dad an orphan at age of 3.

My grandmother tells me that my grandfather Felipe at the time was working for the railroad and had to constantly be on the move repairing railroad tracks, not only routine maintenance but damage caused by the Villistas.

The RR had various gangs (teams or details) of workers and due to them living in close quarters it was not unusual to have man come down sick with the influenza. If one of the workers came down with the illness, they would simply leave him behind with some nurses (not necessarily medically inclined) to care for the person as they had to move on. In occasions there were more than one who would get sick and had to stay behind. It was also not unusual for many to die during the night or shortly after being detected with the decease. In those cases, the corpses of the dead would be buried right away and was usually done close by. If the location was close to a village or town, the local church would usually have a cemetery that could be used. Otherwise, if they were out in the rural area the closes place would do.

On one occasion one of the crew members got sick while they were away from the city and after the man had died some of the men dug a hole close by to the railroad tracks. Mean time other men built a wooden casket. Caskets were not always available or used. At times a simple blanket was used, or the person just laid on the ground (hole) as he was. Wood was not always easily available.

At this time my grandfather was part of the burial detail and didn't personally know the man who had died. Grandfather was told that the man had died during the night and since no embalming was ever done, the burial had to be done right away. Before noon time the hole was dug, and the man was brought over and placed in the casket that had been built and lowered down to the hole. Someone who knew the dead man said some prayers at a small ceremony.

While shoving dirt unto the casket for a while someone yelled to stop and listen. Everyone stopped and listened for a minute. Muffled sounds and faint screams along with some pounding could be heard coming from the casket which had already been half buried with dirt. Everyone froze for a brief time as if making sure they weren't imagining things. Someone yelled "he is alive, get him out" and a couple of man jumped down the hole landing on top of the casket. Being that there was hardly any room to stand around the casket to dig the dirt already on top, some men had to stand on top of the casket and try removing the dirt with their hands as there was only a few inches between the sides of the casket and the dug wall. It took a while before they could uncover the casket enough to try and break the wooden planks to get to the buried person. Finally, after a while they broke through the casket, but by this time the man who apparently had been alive when buried had suffocated and had died.

The man's fingernails and hands had blood on them from where the fingernails had been broken when the man inside the casket had tried to get out by scratching and pounding on the wooden casket. The poor man's face was that of shock and fright. The man's eyes were wide open as well as his mouth as he was gasping for air, and he was laying sideways.

All signs of life were now gone from the body and having nothing more they could do; they went ahead and reburied the now dead man for a second time. No one said a word, they just fill up the hole with dirt.

However, grandfather said he had learned one thing, always make sure the dead are dead before you bury them.

STORY 12

BEAUTY AND THE BEAST

The following story I heard various times from different persons related to my wife. Some were actual witnesses and others although not eyewitnesses to all events, were eyes witness to one or incidents. Yet others where close by when the events took place and heard certain things or saw patrial activity as they were not permitted to be present.

This story involves one of my wife's cousins who was a few years older than her and at the time was in her teens. My father-in-law and mother in-law as well as many of my wife's cousins, aunts and uncles were all witnesses to the events as they occurred at the Hacienda de los Remedios where they all lived at the time. My wife was only about eight years old at the time but can recall some of the things that she saw and heard. Some of the things my wife saw were very scary,especially since she was only eight-year-old, and she says she will never forget.

My wife's cousin was named Ofelia. Ofelia was a very beautiful girl and was around sixteen years old when this took place. As mentioned above the whole family lived in La Capilla de los Remedios (mentioned in stories 8 and 9) in the State of Chihuahua. This happened around 1952.

Ofelia being a very beautiful girl with deep brown hair, light skin, blue eyes, tall, slim and who appeared to be a little bit older then what she was attracted the attention of many boys from around the area. Not to say that the other cousins were not pretty, but Ofelia just stood out.

One day out of the clear blue sky while Ofelia was sitting outside, she suddenly went into what seemed like a trance. Ofelia just sat there wide eyed and staring straight ahead. After a few seconds she started pinching her face so hard that the skin was turning red where she was pinching it. Her mother who was close by observed this and asked her what was wrong, but Ofelia didn't reply. Her mother kept telling her to stop and tried holding her hands back, but Ofelia persisted.

Ofelia would not respond and would fight her mother who was trying to forcibly keep her from hurting herself by holding her hands. Her mother started to become worried and yelled at her husband. Her husband came over running after hearing the panic yell and upon seeing what was happening tried keeping Ofelia from hurting herself. A struggle pursued both the mother and father trying to keep Ofelia from hurting herself when all of a sudden, she got up and started to run around like a wild woman screaming and yelling making strange sounds. Her father and mother tried to stop her and hold her down, but she was too strong for them. By now others had heard or seen the commotion and ran over to help. For the most part they were all relatives who lived close by, and a couple of other cousins and uncles showed up right after.

It took four to five grown men to hold her down as she screamed in a loud voice, wiggled and kicking to set herself free. Her screams were those of fright and she would yell "the snake, the snake" and other times she would yell "the spider, the spider" and she would act as if she was trying to brush something off of her body as if she had snakes or spiders on her person. Her movements and actions were those of a frantic person trying to get rid of the insects on her body.

No one knew what to do except to hold her down to keep her from hurting herself. Her mother kept asking her over and over again what was wrong. Her mother than ran inside the house and got some holy water and started to smear it about her face and body while some of the other women started to pray out loud.

This went on for some time until she started to calm down. Once she calmed down, she would lay for a while all exhausted.

Afterwards Ofelia couldn't remember anything that had happened. She had bruises on her face and about her body from where they had held her down and from where she had hit herself as she wiggled around the dirt floor. But amazingly by the next day they were all gone.

Days went by without a reoccurring incident. Everybody would talk and wonder what had happened that day. But, a few days later the same thing happened again. And again, it would start with Ofelia going into a trance type stage and then she would start to pinch her face and after a while she would start running around frantically yelling and trying to brush something off of herself. This same type of episode kept occurring on and off for months. No one knew why this was occurring or if it would eventually stop or if it was to continue. Her parents did their best to never leave her alone in case it should occur again. The older women would have prayer meetings hoping that it would help especially since there was no church or priest in La Capilla to obtain some spiritual guidance. The closes church was in Cuauhtémoc which was about thirty miles away.

On one occasion while going through one of her episodes a bed sheet was used to wrap around her and hold her down to minimize the injuries. Thinking that this was the best way to keep her from hurting herself and at the same time it would help those holding her down. But Ofelia had such strength that she tore the sheet to pieces. Every time an episode occurred it would take four to five strong men to hold her down. And as before she would make strange noises and scream and seemed to see things. On one occasion my wife said that a parliament of owls came down to the porch and set there just watching. One of the ladies went outside and threw holy water at them but they just jumped from one side to the other.

It was believed in those days (and even now in some places) that witches turn into owls, and they are a bad omen. On another occasion some black crows came down and set on the wires outside the house (Crows are also believed to be related to evil) and again holy water was thrown at them, and they just moved from one side to the other avoiding the holy water as if laughing at those throwing the water at them.

All that could be done at the time was to pray whenever she got one of these trances, now being called seizures by the older folks. These seizures would occur anytime, anywhere. Ofelia was never left by herself in fear that she might go into one of her episodes and hurt herself. As soon as she started to stare and pinch her face, they knew an episode was coming on. The younger children, including my wife, were quickly either taken inside the house or were placed in another room while this went on. My wife remembers being with her other younger cousins in a room while the commotion went on during one of her seizures. They were all in the other room and although they were all afraid, they still tried to see through a crack on the door to see what was going on.

After one of these seizures everyone would be careful not to mention anything to Ofelia. In a way, the younger cousins were scared of her, not knowing what was going on and why she acted the way she did. Most tried to avoid her.

Finally, Ofelia was taken to a nearby village or Hacienda where her parents had been told a lady by the name of Cuca Valeta lived and that she could help Ofelia. The general consensus by now was that this had to involve some type of witchcraft. Ofelia's parents were told that Cuca cured people of witchcraft and other evil spells. Some people referred to her as a Good Witch or White Witch. Cuca spend many hours with Ofelia and was able to cure her of the so-called seizures.

It was later learned that there was a boy who lived in another village close by who was in love with Ofelia. Cuca even mentioned the boy by name. It was learned that Ofelia had rejected his advances as she didn't care much for the boy. He had once asked Ofelia to marry him, but she refused saying that she didn't want to get married yet. The boy became very angry at her rejection and told Ofelia that she was going to regret it, that she was going to be sorry. That if she couldn't be his, she wasn't going to belong to anyone else. Ofelia just brushed it off and went about her business not paying any attention or placing any importance to what he had said.

Cuca said that the boy had used the services of a Black Witch who had placed a spell on Ofelia. And had she not obtained any help, although the spell was not intended to be mortal, it could have been.

Ofelia was cured and never had another reoccurring episode again and she would never recall any of it. But my wife said everyone else did. All of the family was more traumatized then she was. Even today my wife cannot recall what happened without getting goose bumps. Ofelia grew up and would die years later in an automobile accident.

STORY 13

THE LOST SOUL
AT CHRISTO REY

In February 1969 I was discharged from active duty and given orders
to report to the Naval Reserve at my hometown of El Paso Texas.
After serving five and half years in the navy, four years 9 months
aboard the U.S.S. Constellation CVA 64 (an aircraft carrier) I was
being processed to go home. My hitch in the Navy was due to
be completed in July 1969 and since the ship was headed for the
Gulf of Tonkin (Vietnam) to conduct air strikes and was going to
be deployed for nine months everyone with 6 months or less was
discharged from active duty and transferred to the reserve to finish
off one's obligation. I had made four previous tours (they were
called Westpac)cruises during my hitch and engaged in conducting
operations off of Viet Nam. I had married during my last two years
of service and during this time my wife Gloria had made a promise
that should I return unharmed from Viet Nam that we would both
make a pilgrimage up Christo Rey as gratitude.

Christo Rey is a mountain located at the corner of Old Mexico,
New Mexico, and Texas. A huge cross of Christ the King was built
on the top. I believe it was built in the late forties or early fifties. The
cross is situated at the very top of the mountain. A three-mile-long

winding path leads one to the top. It's a small path about 6 feet wide with dirt and small pebbles.

Many religious people make yearly pilgrimages up the mountain to thank our Lord for various wishes granted. Yet, others will go up the mountain for the fun of it, just to get fresh air and exercise. It's a beautiful sight from the top of the mountain and like I mentioned before, you are able to see two countries and three States from up there.

There are no houses or building close to where the starting point is. The closes house being about a quarter of a mile away. So, everyone has to drive up to the starting point on a dirt road and park. You can always know when someone is climbing because of the parked cars. Outside of those visible parked cars which belong to the hikers, you won't see anything or anyone with the exception of an occasional lonely flying hawk or a Border Patrol Unit. If there are no hikers, then the area will be empty, alone, and quiet.

My wife Gloria and I made the drive out there one morning a few weeks after I had arrived home from the Navy. We decided it was best not to wait and make the climb to pay off her promise before any more time went by. When we arrived, there was not a single car or person to be seen around. I assumed it was because it was a weekday, and most people are out working. After we parked, we started walking up the mountain and soon we were going around and around on the small trail. As we walked the only sound, we could ear was the crushing sound of the gravel at our feet caused by our walking. I had an arm around my wife and on occasions we would lean forward a little as we climbed especially on steep up grades. After a while we started to breathe a little harder and the climbing was becoming more difficult. It seemed easy from the bottom but half ways up there you started to feel the incline.

About half ways up the mountain during one of the turns we observed a man walking in front of us in a slow pace. We quickly caught up with him and passed him. As I mentioned before the path is only about six feet wide, so when you pass each other, you are relatively close to each other and can observe the other person if you want. But in this case neither my wife nor I made any effort to say anything to the person we were passing or to look at him. Not till later did I wonder why. Especially since its customary to greet the other person and my wife is very good at greeting people even if she doesn't know them. And it's our Mexican custom and besides it's the proper thing to do.

I did however notice by a quick glimpse through the corner of my eyes that it was a young man in his late teens or early twenties, and he appeared very neat and cleanly dressed with well pressed khaki pants and a solid-colored long sleeve shirt buttoned all the way to the top. I never did see his face, nor did I make an effort to see it, but did however notice he had short black hair neatly combed straight back and he had shiny black shoes. His dress attire was typical of what we used to dress back in the 1960's when I was a kid and before I joined the Navy. (People sometimes called as Cholos) Just for an instant I did wonder why someone would come dressed like that for such a tormenting walk. Nevertheless, we just continued walking and before long we had left him behind.

We finally approached the end of the trail where one has to go single file for the last ten yards or so to where the cross is. I helped my wife as she was already tired, and we stepped into a small altar area that has been built so that people can kneel and pray. There is enough room for about a dozen people in the alter area.

We had barely settled down and in the process of kneeing when I observed that the man, we had passed earlier was now coming up the small entry area. My wife took out her rosary and we started to pray. The young man came into the alter area and kneeled about six feet to my right and just a little behind me on my blind side. Even if I wanted to look at the man, I was unable to do so without turning my head all the way around. All the time we prayed I didn't hear him say anything. The man just kneeled there with his head bowed down.

Finally, we finish the rosary and we stated to leave. The young man stayed behind in a kneeling position with his head down as we left, and no words were exchanged between us.

My wife and I started making the spiraling trip down the mountain talking only once in a while of things we wanted to do with our lives as well as the walk itself. A short distance away we again saw the same young man walking down on the path in front of us. My wife looked at me and in a soft voice said something to the affect that how did he get in front of us. I explained that it was possible to make a short cut by climbing straight down from one path to the lower path. Many people would do this to get down faster. The promise is to climb up, once you have climbed you have done your promise and now you can short cut your way down.

Again, we continued on our descent and again since the young man was walking slower than we were (or we were walking fast) we soon caught up with him. Again, we passed him and this time as we passed, I noticed that the only sound that we could hear was that of our shoes on the gravel path. I tried to concentrate to see if I could hear the man's footsteps, but I heard none. I than got a strange feeling when I realized that the man was making no noise as he walked. I decided not to say anything as I didn't want to alarm my wife. I was tempted to turn around and take a look at the man but felt it would be best not to. Besides I was kind of afraid of what I would see or if the man might say anything to me.

When we finally got to the base of the mountain, I kept looking around for another automobile but only ours was visible. My wife looked up the mountain and said" did you notice something about that man?" "What?" I said. He made no sound on the gravel when he walked. "Wow" I said, I thought I was the only one who noticed that. "No" my wife said," I noticed when we passed him, but I was afraid to say anything "she said.

My wife and I mentioned this to my parents afterwards. My mother said it was probably a poor soul in need of someone to pray for him or maybe that soul had made a promise to climb Christo

Rey and was never ever able to accomplish it while alive and needed our help.

After hearing this for some reason I always felt that if that was the case, then it would have been some young man who had died in Viet Nam.

And I have often wondered about Richie. Richie was the brother of my brother-in-law and brother to my best friend Pete. We grew up together in the Barrio. Richie was killed in Viet Nam. He was a couple of years younger than me and joined the marine Corps. about two years after I joined the Navy. He used to hang out with us in the neighborhood.

And of course, we dressed that very same way as that man on the mountain was dressed and there was a great physical resemblance now that I think of it.

THE JANITOR IN THE WINDOW

In the early 1990's my brother Felipe was working at Rockwell industries as a janitor. The building was a big building in the industrial complex area located next to the International Airport in El Paso.

The building was two stories high, and the front area had huge glass windows panes. My brother was part of a small maintenance crew and would stay late cleaning the machinery and general clean up. Once finished he would lock up at night making sure he was the last person out. There had been another janitor previously named Richard who had worked with my brother but had died a couple of years prior. They were close as they would sit and talk during breaks.

My brother's daughter would regularly come and pick my brother from work and would park the car in the front parking lot facing the building. This enabled my brother to look out the big picture windows and check if his daughter was there. His daughter was also able to see her dad looking out towards the parking lot. There she would wait until her father exited the building through the large front glass doors.

One evening while Chelis (Araceli) my brother's daughter waited in the parking lot for her father, she observed a man standing and looking out from the second-floor area through one of the glass windows. This was the same area her father would usually appear to look out towards the parking lot to see if she was there yet. The windows were so big that a person's complete figure could be observed. The man just stood there with his hands on his hips looking towards the parking lot. Chelis observed the man for a few minutes who didn't seem to move so she just simply disregarded the man and took her focus away from him not thinking much about it. Chelis knew it was not her father and thought that maybe Richard had been replaced by a new janitor.

Shortly after, the lights in the building went out and her father came out of the building. As Felipe was getting into the car Chelis asked him" Where you up on the second floor looking out?" "No" Felipe says "Why?" Chelis then tells her father that she had observed a man looking out of the second-floor windows shortly before the lights went out and he exited the building. Felipe then told Chelis that there was nobody in the building that he was the only one there. Felipe asked Chelis to describe the man and she said the man was about fifty, he was wearing a black tee shirt a black jacket, slick black hair comb towards the back and was standing with his hands on his hips." Oh Shut "Felipe says, that was Richard!

Felipe would later say that in various occasions after the death of Richard which had been from a self-induced drug overdose, many of the other workers had claimed to have seen and heard strange things around the building. But most stories were disregarded and laughed at. Felipe had never personally seen or heard anything but many of the other people claimed that they had.

Felipe and Richard worked together for many years before Richards's death and Richard always dressed the same way and had a strange way of standing with his hands on his waist.

STORY 15

THE LITTLE BOY
AT THE WINDOW

Around the mid 1980's my parents moved to Socorro Texas after years of living in the City of El Paso for many years. They had bought some land and had built a house in an area that used to be a cotton fields. This was a newly developed area and there were no neighbors yet and many of the lots had not yet been sold. The plots sold were one-acre lots which allowed people to bult far apart from each other.

It had taken my parents are brothers some time to build the house as they worked on it mainly on weekends. Once the house was finished, they moved in leaving behind the house where most of us children had been born and my parents and grandparents had lived in since the 1930's.

By now most of us children had grown up and moved out of the house, with the exception of the three youngest boys Charlie (Carlos) and Eddie (Eduardo) and Junior (Demecio). My brother Eddie was the youngest of the three. The new house was a four-bedroom house built in the acre lot as mentioned before and there were very few neighbors and those who were living in the newly developed neighborhood lived some distance away. The whole acre had been fenced in with one small pedestrian gate in front and one vehicle gate on the side which usually remain closed.

It wasn't until years later when I was collecting stories for this book that Eddie would tell me this story.

Eddie said that he didn't like to tell this story because even now just thinking about it gave him the creeps. When this took place, Eddie was not married and lived with my parents, Charlie, and Junior. Eddie had his own bedroom with a large picture window looking towards the side of the yard. The closes neighbor to that side was about fifty yards away. The windows were low enough to where a person could stand outside, and you could see them from the waist up. Eddies bed was right next to the window.

Eddie says that he got home late one night after being out partying and went to bed. He doesn't know how long he had been asleep when he felt someone pulling his blanket down towards his feet. The pull was like tugs and were strong jerking pulls to the point they were violent. Eddie sat up in a half awaken condition to see what was going on. For a moment Eddie thought it was one of his brothers messing with him. Eddie looked towards his feet and there was no one there and the blanket was only covering half of him. There was already enough light in the room to show that it was daybreak, but everything was still quiet as it was very early. For some unknown reason Eddie felt as if there might be something at the window and he turned around to take a look and he saw a boy about six year's old standing on the outside looking in and staring at Eddie through the window. Eddie became so frightened at this that he quickly laid himself back down and covered himself up to his face and rolled himself into a ball with his back towards the window. Eddie did not move nor dared to get up until he was able to hear some familiar voices inside the house side indicating the family was getting up.

No children were living in the area at that time.

Eddie says that the quick glance at the boy and the feeling he had really frightened him. Eddie didn't dare tell anyone of what he had seen, afraid that they would laugh at him. Eddie never saw that kid again but of course he would never look towards that window unless it was really necessary, afraid he might see something there. There were times when Eddie would wonder if in fact, he had seen what he saw, but he says he know he did.

STORY 16

THE SPOTLIGHT
IN THE DARK

Another unexplainable incident that happened to my brother Eddie occurred in 1993. Eddie was married by now and was living in Deming New Mexico. Eddie worked for a mining company out of Playas New Mexico. Every day him and another coworker would make the long drive to work which was some 75 miles distance away from Deming. It would take them approximately one and a half hour or less all depending on road conditions and how fast they could go. They would drive west on Interstate 10 then they would cut south on highway 149 towards Playas. This whole area is mostly desert with an occasional ranch here and there.

On one occasion while traveling at night and on highway 149 between Interstate 10 and Hachita, Eddie who was on the passenger seat turned to look towards the desert area and saw what seemed like a spotlight about one hundred yards off the road at eye level. Eddie mentioned this to his friend who was driving and who turned over and also saw the light. They were commenting as to what that light could be as they traveled through here every day and had never seen it before. There were no roads, houses, or anything else in that area, just bare desert.

As they were talking and looking at the light, the light took off at a very high rate of speed parallel to the ground in the same direction they were traveling and before they were able to say anything the light started to change into different colors and suddenly it burst into sparkles and disappeared.

Eddie and his friend both looked at each other in amazement and said, "did you see that?"

Neither one had any idea what it could have been. Needless to say, every night they would keep their eyes open to see if they could see it again, but they never did.

They mentioned it once to some coworkers and they all laughed at them saying "so how many beers had you guys been drinking?"

STORY 17

A VISIT FROM GRANDPA

As I mentioned previously my parents build a home in Socorro and moved from their home in El Paso where they had lived for over fifty years. The old home was then sold to my brother Felipe and his wife Martha.

In the summer of 2015 one of my brothers thought it would be a clever idea if all my brothers could go camping for a weekend at Silver Lake at the Mescalero Indian Reservation in New Mexico. Our family has been going there for years, but this time it was only going to be males and five of us had agreed. The trip was scheduled for a weekend in June. Some of the nephews were also going to able to accompany us.

In the group was Andres Talamantes who was at the time 22 years old. Andres and his brother Mikey (who was killed in a car accident a few years later) are actually sons of my brother Felipe's wife's sister. However, they were raised alongside the other nephews and for a long time lived at my brother Felipe's house and since they don't have a father, they see Felipe as their dad.

While sitting over the campfire one night and as usual, it wasn't long before scary stories started to lead the conversations. Mikey then tells Andy, tell them about you seeing grandpa. They had grown up seeing my father as their grandfather. My father always treated them as just two more grandchildren. My father had passed away in 1998 when Andy was around 4 or 5 years old. Andy was hesitant at first and finally said that there were a lot of details he had since forgotten. But the best he could recall it happened when he was around 4 or 5 years old (shortly after my dad had died) and that he would frequently see grandpa at the house and that every time he saw him for some unknown reason, he would run a hide from grandpa. He would hide under the table or behind a sofa or whatever. Andy said that grandpa would converse with him, but he could no longer remember the conversation or anything else that happened. He just remembers seeing grandpa and on occasions telling his mom about it, but she never really did anything or commented about it as far as he could recall. It was more like 'yea, okay" and disregard it.

Andy said he saw grandpa quite a few times as he played around the house. Sometimes grandpa would talk to him yet other times he would just be there looking at him. It just seemed like one day it all suddenly stopped, and he no longer saw grandpa.

Many times, he would just simply keep it to himself as no one at the house seemed to care. He wasn't afraid or anything and he thinks he was aware that he was dead, but it just didn't seem to matter at the time.

While talking about the subject, Andres (another Andres) Sanchez who is married to Felipe's daughter Aracely and who also lives at the old house with Felipe, started to tell us about another episode, this one involving his daughter.

Andres has two daughters, one named Jasmin who at the time he told us the story was 8 years old and her sister Mia who was 6 years old. Andres mentioned to us that when Mia was about 3-4 years old on one occasion, she was playing in the living room when her grandmother (My brother Felipe's wife Martha) who was about to seat on a recliner. As she was about to sit down Mia yells, "Don't seat there, can't you see that the man and his dog are there?" "Where?" Martha asked. "There at the seat" Mia says pointing at the recliner. "He has a dog?" Martha asked "yes!" Mia replies. "Well, tell them to leave because I don't like dogs inside the house" Martha tells her playfully thinking that Mia is just simply playing.

Mia then walks up to the front door, opens it, and says,looking at the direction of the recliner "you have to go, grandma doesn't like dogs in the house" after a few minutes of standing there with the door open, Mia, closes the door and goes back to her playing as if nothing had happened. Martha then asked Mia, "what kind of dog was it?" "Oh, it was a small dog "Mia replies, in a matter of fact like.

However, Martha after thinking about it later tells her husband (Felipe) and her daughter (Mia's mother) about the incident. The more they talk about it and ask Mia more questions of what she had seen, the more they were convince it was my dad. (Mia's great grandfather) They showed a picture of my dad who had died before Mia was born and asked her if that was the person she had seen. (She never knew my dad in person). She identified the picture as the same man she saw in the living room. This was the same house and area where Andy had seen my dad years earlier.

My Father (Mia's great grandfather) did have a dog. The dog's name was Prince. Price was a funny looking dog as it had the body and face of a German Sheppard,but with short little legs. I have never seen a dog like that. That dog was very close and very faithful to my dad and would always follow my dad everywhere he went. You could always see them together around the property where my dad lived. After my dad passed away and after the funeral, we came back home to fine that Price had also passed away. He was found by the back door laying there dead. No explainable reason for his death.

The house where all of this happened had been built by my grandfather in the 1930's. With the exception of my brother and I who saw a man in the alley way one night, to my knowledge no one else has ever seen anything like this at the house since then.

STORY 18

THE SHADOW ON THE WALL

During the summer of 2015, a month after I camped out with my brothers and nephews at Silver Lake New Mexico, my wife and I returned to Silver Lake with my son Marco, his wife and my three grandkids for a few days of camping.

Two days later a co-worker of Marco named Jesse Martinez and his wife Becky, and their three children also came up to camp at Silver Lake. They parked their trailer close to Marco's and later that night joined us at our campfire. It was then that Marco my son introduced his friend Jesse and his family to us. As we sat around the fire and got to know each other, I asked if they had ever experienced some type of unusual event in their life. I told them about the book I had plans to write on collection of strange stories.

Jessie said he didn't believe in supernatural stuff, but his wife said that she did believe and that she had experienced unusual events when she was growing up. She went on to say that she seldom spoke of what she had experienced as a child and mainly because her husband didn't believe in that sort of thing, and she was afraid that people would not believing her and of being laughed at. I assured her that my personal experiences and in talking to other persons had convinced me that supernatural things do exist. I told her of some of the stories that I had been told and of firsthand experiences.

61

After a while, once she felt more comfortable, and assured she then went on to tell us the following story.

Becky said she was around eight or nine years old and lived with her parents and two brothers in a rental home close to the Isleta area. The house was an older home in the vicinity of the Ysleta High School in El Paso's lower valley area. Becky said that she recalls her mom always frequently speaking of a shadow appearing on the walls and how she believed it was a shadow of an old lady. However not much discussion evolved around it, and with time it was hardly mentioned.

One day Becky says she was sitting in her bedroom in front of her dresser which had a large mirror when she felt as if someone was looking at her from the hallway. She glanced in the mirror from where you could see the hallway towards her back and to her surprise, she saw the reflection of a figure which looked like that of a person. And in fact, it did resemble that of old lady as there were certain features and details that lead one to believe that. She immediately remembered what her mom had said about seeing a shadow of a woman.

The shadow figure was the size of a normal person even if you couldn't see certain details, you could see very clearly that it was a figure of a human. Becky was sure she was seeing the figure of the old lady her mom had mentioned. Becky became so frightened that she stood up and ran out of the room.

This was the first time she saw the shadow figure herself and she also knew that other family members had seen "the old lady", especially her mother.

She also recalls that at times the family would be sitting down in the living room watching TV, and you could hear the sound of breaking glass coming from the dining room. Everyone would jump up and run to the kitchen to see what it was and to their surprise all windows were intact and there was no broken glass anywhere to be seen. Not on the floor or anywhere else.

Becky says this happened more than once and every time they

would all get scared as if it was the first time. It was something you don't become accustomed to. Her mother would sometimes go to the point that she would seem to go into a trance and talk to the old lady. Becky recalls one occasion when the family was having dinner in which her mother seemed to go in a trance and would actually have a conversation with someone that wasn't physically there with them.

Family members would try to talk to her mom, and she would ignore them. Finally, her father would grab her form the shoulders and shake her calling her name out loud and her mother would become angry saying "can't you see I'm talking to the Lady?" No one would say anything more and continued eating.

But Becky does believe her mother was talking to someone even if that person wasn't there for everyone to see. Her mom would not say what was spoken between her and old the lady as it was difficult to tell what she was saying cause it sounded mumbled.

Becky recalls hearing that the house used to belong to some old lady, who she believed died at that home. How the death occurred they don't know.

After a long time of these occurrences happening to many members of the family, Becky says they started to ignore the shadow and just went on as if nothing. With time no one seemed to be afraid of it anymore. After all, the shadow of the old lady didn't seem to do any harm to anyone.

STORY 19

THE HUNTED BEDROOM

The following incident occurred to my wife Gloria and our grandson Marco Antonio II who was four years old at the time of the occurrence. My wife and grandson were visiting our son Marco a Border Patrol agent stationed in Brackettville Texas at the time and working out of that station but was actually living in Uvalde with a friend named Donny who was also a Border Patrol agent. Both Marco and Donny would commute every day to Brackettville from Uvalde which was not too far.

Donny was originally from Uvalde and had a home there and was allowing Marco to stay with him. It was an older home but had all that Donny needed who was not married and lived by himself. He had a girlfriend who would on occasions also stay there.

Marco was divorced and had monthly as well as yearly visitation rights with his son Marco II. Marco II lived with his mom in El Paso. Due to the distance monthly visitations for the most part were not exercised by Marco. However, the yearly summer visitation was a whole month long. My wife Gloria would accompany Marco II and babysit while Marco was at work during these summer visitations.

During one of these two-week summer visitation rights in 2006 my wife Gloria as usual accompanied Marco II during this two-week visitation. It was the first time my wife had gone since big Marco had moved in with Donny. Prior to that Marco had been living by himself in an apartment.

As I mentioned Little Marco was about four years old at the time. Donny's old house was a two-bedroom house with a living room and kitchen dining area combination. Donny's girlfriend was named Julianita (but called Julie) and she would frequently visitor Donny's house to the point that she had her own key.

The day that Marco, my wife, and Little Marco arrived in Uvalde from El Paso to start the two-week visitation period, Marco dropped them off at the house and left to buy some food for the two week stay.

My wife Gloria then tells the story that while big Marco was gone to the store, she and little Marco started to go into what was Marco's bedroom and as they were about to enter little Marco hesitated and started to cry. My wife also got a cold chill and she quickly picked little Marco up in her arms and they walked down the hall towards the living room not wanting to go into the bedroom. The bedroom was a decent size bedroom but only had a small cot where Marco slept and a small couch. There was also a large closet and Marco's work clothes and other work stuff that he used was laying on the floor against the wall in the closet.

It is unknown why they both felt that way when they started to enter the bedroom, but they did.

My wife and little Marco waited in the living room area till Marco returned from the store. Once Marco returned my wife felt it would be best not to say anything of what had occurred. My wife Gloria quickly prepared some food for them, and they sat down to eat.

After eating they went into the Marcos bedroom, but this time Marco accompanied them and although my wife says she still felt strange it was not as bad. Little Marco who was being held by his dad in his arms also didn't react. My wife kept thinking that maybe it was just her and that there was nothing to be frightened about. At least she kept telling that to herself trying to shake it off.

Soon Donny and Julianita showed up and she and Julianita were introduced, and they all sat around and talked all evening. Later that night my wife asked Marco why he hadn't bought a bedroom set, that little Marco didn't like the small cot he was using and had even cried when he first saw it. Marco then told my wife to go ahead and look around the next day for a bedroom set. The night passed without any incident.

The next day Julianita and my wife found a nice used bedroom set and had it delivered. By the time Marco came home from work they had a new bedroom set. That evening while big and little Marco were playing in the new bed my wife had set a glass of water on top of the dresser and she saw the glass move. Upon seeing the glass move my wife said in a load voice "Ave Maria purísima" and she asked Marco "Did you see the glass move!" but Marco simple turned around looked at my wife, the glass and went back to wrestling and playing with little Marco as if nothing.

The next day after Donny and Marco had gone to work, Julianita came over and she was going to take my wife to find some curtains for the bedroom. While together my wife told Julianita of the glass moving and Julianita asked her if, she was sure. Maybe you just imagined it she would say. Donny has lived there for a long time, and I go there all the time at different hours of the day and night, and we have never seen or heard anything she said. My wife was sure of what she had seen but at this point found it useless to continue the conversation.

Later on, Julianita was helping my wife put the curtains on the bedroom window when they heard the front door open, and slam shut and what sounded like footsteps and some bags hitting the floor. This was a customary routine for Marco and Donny. Every day when they got home; they would toss the bags they carried on the floor. My wife then told Julianita (who had also heard the door slam)" oh, the boys just got here; they must have gotten off early today." Both my wife and Julianita went out of the bedroom to greet the boys and went into the living room area but there was no one there. Julianita turned to look at my wife with a questionable look and my wife herself had a puzzled face and for a few seconds no one spoke. Neither one could believe what had just happened and they questioned themselves if they had really heard something or if they had imagined it. Now Julianita was also having her doubts.

Needless to say, they told the boys when they got home of what had occurred and after laughing at them for a while but saw how serious they were and just shrugged their shoulders as if to say,well!

My wife stayed there for the whole two weeks and although she felt some chills at times and was scared most of the time, nothing else really happened again.

She did however say that she constantly prayed and asked the Lord and our Holy Lady to help her keep calm and not see or hear anything anymore.

Julianita did come every day and spend as much time as she could with my wife and little Marco to keep them company while Marco and Donny were out working. Soon the visitation was over with, and they came back home.

THE TALKING SKELETON

This following story comes from Manuelita the mother of my daughter in law Irene. Manuelita and her family are from Sonora Mexico, and they grew up around a small town known as Nacozari de Garcia.

Manuelita went on to say that she had an uncle named Cruz who for many years claimed to have heard a story about a buried treasure which was buried close by to Nacozari. According to her uncle various attempts had been made to locate this treasure but nobody had located it. It was unknown how far back this story of the buried treasure goes; it had been passed on from generation to generation.

One day her uncle and a friend were out drinking and talking about this buried treasure which according to the legend was protected by a skeleton. This skeleton would have to give permission to anyone looking for the treasure in order for that person to continue and eventually find the treasure.

Almost everyone around the area knew the approximate location of the buried treasure, but everyone feared to venture there. One of the reasons was the fact that the skeleton would have to be confronted first and it was unknown what would happen in the event the skeleton did not appreciate the intrusion, so the rumor went.

As her uncle Cruz and his friend continued to talk and drink about this legend and the more beer they drank, the braver they got. Finally, when they were drunk, they dared each other to go to the place and look for the skeleton. Of course, her uncle would later say that he never really believed in the story and had decided to go ahead simply because of the dare and the alcohol plus being sure that nothing was going to be found. He just went for the fun.

Anyway, that evening her uncle and his friend after consuming set off to the mentioned area which was close by. Her Uncle Cruz wanted to show to his friend that there was no such thing as a skeleton nor treasure. Once they got to the location and after walking for a short distance up some hills it started to get dark. His friend was having second thoughts and wanted to go back. "No "said her uncle Cruz, "we are going to continue until we meet this *#@+ skeleton ".

About then they observed a light in the distance and as it got closer, they realized it was a walking skeleton coming in their direction and it had a small light inside of the rib area. Cruz at the time thought it was some joke someone was playing and figured he would get closer and disrobe the person wearing the custom.

However, as Cruz and his friend got closer, and he was able to observe the skeleton closer he realized it was an actual skeleton and felt fear for the first time. Cruz threw himself to the ground face down with arms starched out forming a cross with his body and closing his eyes. Cruz then yelled out" in the name of Jesus I ask you are you from this world or from the other" the skeleton replied, "from the other," "Go away" her uncle said. "Take my hand" the skeleton said, "and I will lead you to the treasure"," no, no" her uncle said, "I will not hold your hand, and I ask you in the name of God to depart and let us be."

Her uncle Cruz knew that according to legend should he hold the skeleton's hand, the skeleton would take him away forever. "Then come back tomorrow at eleven and I will lead you to the treasure" the skeleton said.

There was silence after that and after a while her uncle Cruz, who was still lying face down paralyzed trembling with fear was able to gather enough strength to get his body to move and he got up and run away with his friend following close behind who had also been laying down with their faces covered with their hands.

Never again did her uncle go back to that place or anywhere close to it. Her uncle Cruz never disbelieved other legends and myths that he was told after that.

According to Manuelita her uncle seldom if ever spoke about the incident. He would always tell young relatives "Never doubt nor challenge legends."

STORY 21

THE BIRD FROM HELL

I first met Araceli, my daughter-in-law's sister during the Holidays of December 2013. She and her family had come down from Sonora Mexico to visit for the Holidays. We had gathered in my house to celebrate one evening and after dinner we were all sitting around conversing. Irene my daughter in law was aware that I was drafting this book and told me that I should ask her sister Araceli of what had happened to her when she was younger.

I approached Araceli and asked her, but she refused to tell me. She said she didn't like to talk about it. We saw each other on and off for the next few days and every time I had an opportunity, I would ask her about the incident she didn't want to talk about. Finally, one evening she said OK.

Araceli said that it had been such a terrifying event that even now, thirty years later she is still frightened whenever she recalled the incident, and it was something she didn't like to think about. Present with me when Araceli finally agreed to tell the story was her mother, my wife, and other members of her family.

First, she said that when this occurred, she was about seven or eight years old, and she was living with her mother in Nacozari Sonora. Her mother and father were divorced but her father lived a short distance away in the same town. Her mother and father's mother (her grandmother) did not have a good relationship with each other, so she didn't have much of a relationship with her father or his family. However, they did see each other on occasions.

One evening Araceli says she was told by her mother to go and wash the dishes. She was watching one of her favorite Mexican children shows on T.V. at the time and didn't want to move. Her mother told her various times and finally her mother became very angry and yelled at her to go and wash the dishes or else.

Bring that the situation had now become aggravated she angrily got out of the sofa in an angry mood and left the T.V. area stomping her feet on the way to the kitchen. Just before starting to clean the dishes, she felt the urge to go to the rest room to urinate. Since the bathroom was an odd house located in the backyard some distance from the house, she decided to go just outside the back door next to the kitchen.

As soon as she went out the back door and down a couple of steps, she squatted down to relief herself.

While she sat there, she noticed up on an evergreen tree which was located by the side of the house a few feet away some movement up in the branches. She looked up and although it was dark, she was still able to make out a big bird about the size of a big turkey. Although she couldn't clearly see many of the features and details, she did notice that the bird was flapping its wings in a slow motion. At first Araceli was not frightened thinking it was just a big bird. She kept looking at the bird and it seemed as if the bird had a head bigger then what a bird should normally have. Suddenly the bird jumped down from the tree towards her and it seemed as if it was going to land on her but landed right next to her only a few feet away. This time Araceli was able to see that the head was larger and almost human like and there were a lot of fleshy growth hanging all over the face. The fleshy growth was like the type of fleshy growth you would normally see on the neck of a turkey. But the scariest thing were the eyes, the eyes were human and were staring straight at her. Araceli was frozen for a few seconds but was finally able to yell and in a panic, she was able to move wanting to get as far away from the creature as far she could. She stood up halfway and begun to push herself backwards leaning and pushing herself on the door as if trying to go through it, to get back inside the house.

She recalls yelling in a panic and wanting to get out of there, but the only way was backwards. She yelled and screamed and stomped her feet and waved her arms up and down and tried covering her face with her hands. In seconds her mother was there talking to her.

Her mother recalls that she had a tough time opening the door to get out and help her because Araceli kept pushing on it with her back. Araceli was yelling, kicking, and running her hands up and down her face in a panic. She was pushing herself so hard against the door that her mother had trouble pushing her off of it.

It took some time to get her calmed down her mother would say. Araceli had scratches all over her face, but it was unknown it the thing had done it or if she had done it herself.

A few days later Araceli would tell her story to her father who would only listen quietly and say "Humm, Humm" while Araceli told him of what had happened. The only words her father would say was "did she scratch you?"

About a week later Araceli came across her half-brother who also lived in the neighborhood. Her half-brother (her father's son) lived with her father and grandmother (father's mother) and was a little bit older than her. Her half-brother asked her if she wanted to go with him to pick some fruit. Their grandmother (her father's mother) had some fruit trees in her back yard, and they would often go over and pick some fruit.

While there Araceli told him the story of what had happened to her when she saw the big bird. After hearing the story, her half-brother said, "that was grandmother, she is a witch." "What?" Araceli would say. "Yes" her brother said.

He then went on to tell Araceli that he was prohibited from saying anything, but that their grandmother was a witch and would often appear in such a way. He further told her not to say anything otherwise he would get in trouble.

Needless to say, Araceli never visited her grandmother again and would always stay clear of her house, fruit, or no fruit.

STORY 22

THE MOTHER-IN LAW WITCH

After Araceli had told me her story (#21), her mother said she wanted to tell me some more about her ex-mother-in-law, Araceli's grandmother.

Manuelita, Araceli's mother told me that it was true that she had never had a good relationship with her mother-in-law.

Manuelita said that she had many problems with her mother-in-law and decided to divorce her husband who seemed to be dominated and greatly controlled by his mother. She knew her mother-in-law never liked her, even more since she refused to be dominated by her.

Soon after leaving her husband, she had become very ill. She had constant hemorrhages that would last for days. She at times would lose so much blood that she was becoming anemic. Home remedies were not doing any good. She went on like that for months and almost a year later she was taken to a town near to Nocozari where she was told about a lady (white witch) who might be able to cure her.

The lady interviewed her, asked many questions, and recommended that she be permitted to give her some treatments. Manuelita agreed. After various treatments with this lady, the lady told her that someone had wished her harm and had put a spell on her, causing the ailment. The lady also said that had she not come over when she did, in a week or two she would have been dead.

The lady asked her if she wanted to know who had caused her this harm and Manuelita said no, that she didn't want to know. The lady said that it didn't really matter and that the spell that that person had placed on her was now going to be reversed. The lady then told her that either way in a couple of days someone in her family was going to have a dream which would disclose the person who had caused her the harm. After the treatments Manuelita felt good and all her ailments went away.

Days later her daughter told her that she had had a dream that her grandmother had stabbed and killed her (Manuelita) with a knife. Manuelita then remembered of what the old lady had told her about one of her family members having a dream and revealing who it was that caused her her harm. However, Manuelita didn't say anything, just kept it to herself.

A day later Manuelita learned that her mother-in-law had died. According to some people who had been by her dead bed, they claimed that her mother-in-law became ill suddenly and after a couple of days died suddenly. No one knew what the cause of her death was. But what was strange was that as the lady lay in bed dying, a small brown owl flew into the room and landed on the headboard of the bed as the lady was dying and sat there until she died then flew away.

No one dared to interfere with the owl, and everybody kept quiet and didn't talk about it.

THE BLACK HAND

This following story was told to me in the late 1950's by Manuel Rosales a cousin of my mother. According to him it happened when he was a teenager growing up in Mexico. Manuel admitted that he was not necessarily a perfect young boy and was constantly giving his mother a hard time. He never mentioned actually what it was that he did or didn't do, but it must have been bad enough that now as a grown man he was ashamed to say so.

Anyway, he went on to say that one evening after having one of his usual fight with his mother he got dressed and prepared to go out in the town to party. His mother would always threaten him by saying that something bad was going to happen to him and that God was going to punish him for being such a misbehaved son. That because he would not listen and was always talking back and not doing what she told him that he was going to pay the price, Manuel would just laugh at her.

This evening as he opened the door that opened into his room to exit his bedroom, the door slammed on him as if a strong wind had pushed the door shut. The only problem there was no wind inside his room. For a second, he was stun. But in a second or two he recovered and again grabbed the doorknob and pulled the door open and again the door shut closed. Again, he grabbed the doorknob and pulled on it with anger and was cursing at the door and again

the door shut on him with such force that it made a loud noise and the wall trembled. At that instance for some unknown reason Manuel glanced at the door and saw an imprint of a black hand on the middle of the door. It was a large man's size hand imprint, and it was clear as day.

Manuel stared at the imprint and started yelling at his mom. Upon hearing Manuel yell in such a panic his mother ran to see what was going on. She got to the outside of the bedroom and upon seeing the door closed turned the knob and pushed it in. She saw Manuel standing there looking at the door with a fixed stare. "What's wrong Manuel?" his mother asked as Manuel started stepping back wards still looking at the door and at the same time pointing at it unable to speak.

Manuel says that he was frozen, he felt a strange feeling, it was more of a frightful feeling, and he couldn't take his eyes off of the imprint. Manuel would say that he had never had such an impressive feeling. His mother would later say that he just kept repeating "The door, the door!" but Manuel can't remember that.

His mother turned and saw the hand imprint and started to pray. As they both stood there the hand gradually started to disappear until eventually it was gone.

Manuel said that after this occurrence many things changed around the house and his life. And it seemed for a long time every time he exited his bedroom, he would glance at the door t make sure nothing was there.

THE GHOST BY
THE CEMETERY

This is another story that Manuel Rosales told me (story 23). He said that years after the hand incident had occurred and when he was in his late teens or early twenties him and his mother now had a very different relationship and things were going well and he now had a job.

This new incident also happened in the same town in Mexico. Manuel said that his new job required him to work late, and he walked to and from his job. It would be dark, and late at night when he got off from work. This job was some distance away from his house and although he could take the public transit to go to work, when he got out there were no longer buses running. So, he would have to walk home.

He would usually get home around eleven o'clock at night and his mother would usually wait up for him and they would talk of the day's events for a while before going to bed.

Manuel would use a short cut to save on time, but it would require him to walk pass an old cemetery which was located alongside one of the main streets. With the exception of about thirty yards of open space at the main entrance of the cemetery, the rest of the cemetery was enclosed with a high adobe wall fence. Part of it ran alongside the sidewalk. The sidewalk was mostly dirt even thought some parts had cement or stones.

Manuel says he never really thought much of the fact that it was a cemetery although at night it was a little spooky, but he had been walking by there for some time and nothing had ever happened, so he had gotten accustomed to it.

However, one evening for some unknown reason as he was walking back home late at night, he felt a little uneasy as he was nearing the accessible area of the cemetery. From this area you could see towards the inside of the cemetery. He doesn't recall ever having such a heavy feeling or worry. However, he felt some relief when he observed a man walking ahead of him, also nearing the entrance area of the cemetery. Manuel speeded up to catch up to the man who was wearing a long overcoat which went down passed his knees. The man was also wearing a black hat and the collar from the coat was folded up as if being used for protection from the chilly wind. This was very common in those days and in the town, so Manuel didn't give it a second thought.

Manuel caught up to the man and slowed down just behind him. Manuel than started walking right behind and to the side of the man on the sidewalk area which had cement and rock floor and he felt more secure since he was no longer alone.

In the silence of the night Manuel noticed that he could hear his footsteps on the rock surface sidewalk, but not the man's. Manuel concentrated to make sure he was right on the footsteps and at the same time looked down at the man's feet and saw that the man had no legs and was simply floating on the air as it moved along. For a second Manuel didn't know if to stop, run or what.

Manuel said that all he could think of what to do was to pray. Manuel started to pray and walk faster and closed his eyes for a second and when he opened his eyes again the man was gone.

Manuel doesn't know if the man went towards the entrance of the cemetery (as he didn't want to look that way) or he simply disappeared.

Manuel said that nothing unusual happened before the incident and he has no idea why he would have encountered that man or who he was or what he wanted.

He continued working at the same place but now he would walk the long way around avoiding the cemetery.

THE UFO OVER
THE LANDFILL

In 1975 I was working with the El Paso Police Department as a patrolman. I was working out of the Police Sub-Station known as the Lower Valley Station. We were responsible for the far east area of the city One evening while assigned to the graveyard shift (11pm-7am) I was assigned to work what was known as district 74 which was the last district on the east side of El Paso above (north) Interstate 10 which was its southern boundary. Its northern boundary was Montana since there was nothing north of there except the airport. The eastern boundary was the end of the city limits. My partner for this night was Officer Ramirez. He was not my regular partner but for some reason we wound up together that night.

The Lee Trevino area had just been developed and there was clearing still being done between Lee Trevino and George Dieter. George Dieter was still a dirt road which ran north and south from Montana. There were no homes yet, but preparations were being made.

We would, when time permitted, check out the desert area. Usually after 2:00 am (after the bars closed) and especially on weekdays everything would become very quiet and calm. We didn't have too many businesses to patrol and check for break-ins, but we did on occasions find stripped stolen cars out in the desert area and illegal dumping.

We would have to drive in the area using some small dirt roads that we had become familiar with and these roads usually zig zagged throughout. The only paved road was Zaragoza which went north from North Loop and curved eastward at present day Montwood, and Loop 375. It then continued eastward to Montana outside the city limits. The other road also paved ran from Montana and present-day Loop 375 and it ran southward passed in front of the land Fill and crossed Zaragoza at present day Loop 375 and Montwood. This road eventually became the frontage road for Loop 375. The road ran all the way to Alameda in a straight line and parallel to Zaragoza. Zaragoza road was a farm road and the whole area north of the freeway was mainly desert.

We would often come across couples who had gone out to the desert to do their thing, we called them lovers, and we would always make sure that the girl was of age and that she was there out of her own free will. Outside of that we really didn't care if consenting adults but did advise them to get a hotel since it was dangerous out in the area.

On occasions (mainly weekends) we would find campfires with booze parties and pot parties or a combination of both and we would break them up after confirming everyone was of age. We also find illegal hunters on occasions and illegal trash dumpers.

The Municipal landfill (trash) was located at present day pebble Hills and Loop 375. On a paved road which laid about two miles east of present-day Lee Trevino. There were no homes there and as I mentioned before this road and Zaragoza were the only two roads and were pretty lonely at night with very little nighttime traffic and pitch-dark.

A few months before this date some of the sanitation workers had found some large plastic bags contacting some human remains cut up in pieces in the landfill. An investigation later revealed that a man whose last name was Valentino had killed and cut up a woman in an apartment on Alameda Street and deposed of the cut-up body parts in bags and had thrown them at the city dump. That case had only given us just one more reason to check for suspicious vehicles around the area.

Around four am in the morning I was driving the police unit and I took a dirt road going east (later became Pellicano) towards Zaragoza from another dirt road (which later became George Dieter). There were various dirt roads around the area and unless you knew the area, one could easily become lost. The dirt roads never went on a straight line, they would always go in a zig sag pattern going around the large mesquite bushes.

As I drove, I was going really slow, and it was a beautiful star filled night. Ramirez was half asleep with boredom as I slowly followed the dirt road looking for any signs of activity on occasions using the spotlight. For some reason I then turned to look north towards the city dump, and I saw a light at the distance. The light looked like a light on a telephone pole, just like you would see on a street corner. It was a yellowish light and it appeared to be right at the dump site which was about a 2 miles from our location. I turned to Ramirez and told him "Look, they put a light at the dump" Ramirez sitting on the passenger side set up a little and bending a little forward to get a better look said "yea, it must be because of the body they found"

We exchanged a couple of comments as I continued to drive and look at the light which by now seemed to be moving. "Hey" I called to Ramirez; the light is moving. The light was coming toward us just as if it was a helicopter hovering and moving very low and slow at the same height.

I lived on an aircraft carrier for over five years, so I had seen a lot of different aircraft to include helicopters flying day and night. I kept looking at the light expecting to see the required stroke light under the aircraft but could not see any. I then rolled down the window of the patrol car so that maybe I could hear the copter blades making their sound, but I couldn't hear anything, and the copter (thing) kept coming closer at the same altitude. To better listen I decided to turn off the patrol car's engine and the police car headlights. I figured the lights might spook the things as it got closer so it would be best to go camouflage in the dark.

However, in the instant I turned off the engine and headlights and as I was looking at the thing, it shot straight up in the air at an unbelievable speed something similar to a 4th of July rocket but much, much faster. I had never seen, nor did I know there was anything that could move that fast. The light (thing) started weaving half ways up the sky then it blinked and flickered a couple of time and then it seemed to disappear and blended in with the starts and disappeared.

I grabbed the mic (police radio) and told Ramirez "I am going to call in." Hold on Ramirez says, what are you going to say? I thought for a second and realized I didn't know what I was going to say. I had grabbed the mic by instinct. The airport is not far I said, and Ft. Bliss is across Montana, someone must have seen something I said. Radar must have picked up that thing on their screen, I said. "I don't know "Ramirez said, at which time I too started to have second thoughts. Well, let's call the sergeant I said. We agreed on that and I called the sergeant to meet us at the Village Inn on Airway by Montana, as it was the only restaurant that was open all night and the closest to us.

We arrived first and while we waited for the sergeant, and I drew what we had seen on a napkin to show the Sergeant. We explained to the Sergeant what took place and as we were talking, he started to give us a grin that only indicated to me, he didn't believe what we were saying. He then started to chuckle, and I told him we were serious and that we were not kidding, that we were very serious. He then realized that we were dead serious.

After listening to us the sergeant thought for a while then recommended that we keep it to yourselves, nobody is going to believe you, he said.

After some coffee and talk both Ramirez and I agreed.

However, years later when ever Ramirez and I crossed paths we would always point at each other and say, "have you seen any UFO'S?"

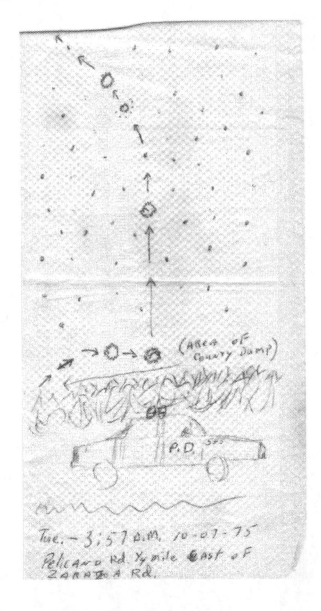

THE UFO OVER SAN JUAN

UFO's are something many people have experienced but seldom ever talk about it. I think there are many more who have witnessed an event then what we suspect.

While gathering material for this book I asked my Comadre who has a doctored in teaching and who was the Principal at Bel Aire High School at the time if she had ever experienced any unusual thing and here is what she had to say.

My comadre and neighbor Dora told me this following story during one of her visits to our house in 2014. Dora said that this incident occurred when she was still a newlywed. Her husband Jessie worked at a trucking company which had their yard off of Clark Street in El Paso Texas. The area is considered as the central part of El Paso, it is highly populated and the neighborhood around there is known as San Juan.

Dora told me that one evening right around sun set she was driving south on Clark Street from Throw bridge to take Jessie his dinner. Dora was nearing the truck yard when all of a sudden, she saw up in the sky, not too high a large disk type object, like the flying saucers you see in the movies. She said the object just hovered with a lighted ring around it and the saucer thing had a dome on top and was very bright. Dora got so scared she stopped on the side of the road to see the thing.

Dora couldn't believe what she was seeing and found it intriguing.

Suddenly while she was staring at the object it just took off straight up at such a high rate of speed and it was gone in a fraction of a second without making any noise.

Dora said it took her a little while to get her composure back and continue her drive. She did tell her husband of the incident but very few others, as after a while she too started to wonder if she had actually seen the thing. It was just a matter of seconds or minutes, and it could have easily been overlooked by many as they go on with their daily lives hardly ever looking upward.

She just happened to be lucky, in a sense that she was able to see the anomaly.

STORY 27

THE VOMITING CURSE

This story was told to me by my God son Oscar. Oscar was born and raised in Chihuahua City Mexico which is located approximately 225 miles south from El Paso Texas. I have known Oscar's parents since I got married to my wife, his mother and my wife are cousin. Ever since Oscar was a toddler and able to be without his mother, he would spend a lot of time with us. Later on, as a teenager he would spend the whole summer months in our home. Oscar would also join us on our vacations and trips. Oscar spends so much time with us that he was able to pick up and learn to speak and read English very well. My son Marco is the same age as Oscar so they would always spend time together and for us it was like having another son.

I was surprised when Oscar told me this story years after it had occurred. I had mentioned to Oscar I was drafting this book and he said he had a story to tell me that had occurred when he was 18 years old. He had never thought about telling his story and he was not sure if his parents had mentioned it to me or not. Oscar was now married now and had his own children.

Oscar went on to tell me that when he was about eighteen years old, for about eight months he had suffered from not being able to keep any food down. Every time he ate something, right away he

89

would throw it up. One thing Oscar did notice was that whenever he physically left the city of Chihuahua, he was okay.

It only occurred while actually at home or at least while within the city. For that same reason he didn't say anything thinking it was something that came and went and that eventually it would go ago.

Oscar said that that same year and while he still had the ailment summer arrived and he came to visit us and spent the summer with us. All the time he was with us he felt fine and had no problem with his throwing up. Oscar never mentioned anything because he felt his illness had been some type of a virus and felt that it had now gone away.

However as soon as he went back home, the ailments started again. He went to three different doctors who gave him a pretty good checkup, but they all told him there was nothing physical wrong with him.

Oscar was losing weight and feeling weak and feeling like not doing anything, not even going to school. Finally, one day, his father after seeing him in such a condition told him that he was taking him to see a Curandero since doctors were unable to fine what was wrong.

Oscar said he had never believed in those things, but he went along anyway. Mainly, Oscar says, because he had no choice. Oscar remembers going into this house which had a bunch of pictures all over the place and lighted candles. Some pictures seemed like pictures of saints. Also, on the floor of one of the rooms was a large painted five-pointed star with lit candles around it.

His father had previously talked to the man, so when he saw Oscar, he knew what the problem was. The man looked at Oscar and told him to stand in the middle of the painted star on the floor. Oscar tried to tell the man of how he felt and what was wrong with him, but the man motioned to him to be quiet. The man told Oscar that he didn't want to hear anything, to just be quiet.

Oscar stood there, in the middle of the star with his arms crossed in front of him and the man told him not to cross his arms or legs in front of him because he couldn't read him. The man told Oscar that he needed to put his arms and hand to the sides of his body and stand still. Oscar did as he was told, and the man brought a full body mirror and set it in front of Oscar. The man than covered Oscar with a white sheet from head to toe. Oscar could hear the man walking around him mumbling saying what sounded like prayers. As the man walked around for a while, he started to describe to Oscar everything that Oscar had felt, down to the smallest detail. Oscar was amazed of how the man knew everything.

After a few minutes the sheet was removed, and the man told Oscar to sit down. The man sat down infront of Oscar and told him that someone had put a spell on him and if he wanted to know who it was. Oscar said yes. The man said it was Alicia (not real name used) and Oscar right away knew who she was. The girl had been Oscar's girlfriend up to sometime ago when he broke up with her. The man asked Oscar if he had had any sexual relation with the girl and Oscar said no. Good, the man said I am going to cure you, but if you had had any sexual relations with this girl there would have been nothing, I could have done for you.

But the man did warned Oscar and told him, don't you *ever* again play with someone's sentiments and emotions. Oscar knew exactly what the man meant

, Oscar says that at that point he knew what the man was talking about. Oscar recalled that when he was going out with this girl, she was madly in love with him and would have done anything for him yet Oscar on the other hand was also going out with another girl.

Oscar admitted that he did take the girl for granted and would often do things that he shouldn't have. Worse, Oscar says that one time both girls learned that Oscar was going out with both of them at the same time. This of course angered both girls. But feeling sure and confident he didn't care.

The man prayed over Oscar touching him over the shoulders and when he was done praying his prayers and doing what he had to do, he asked Oscar how he felt. Oscar replied that he really felt good and, in a way, felt as if a weight had been lifted from him. Oscar asked the man how much he owed him, and the man said nothing that Oscar would have to come back again. The man gave Oscar a liquid to drink for a week and told him when he had finished the drink to come back and see him. A week later Oscar felt cured and would no longer throw up after eating. His father gave Oscar five hundred pesos to take to the witch doctor on the next visit which Oscar did. Oscar never had any more vomiting episodes and within time he forgot about it. Once or twice, Oscar did see this girl around town, and when he did, he would always go out of his way to keep from meeting her.

STORY 28

BOGEY ON THE SOUTH CHINA SEA

While in the Navy in the early 1960's I was stationed onboard the Navy Aircraft Carrier U.S. S. Constellation CVA64. I had reported on board in May 1964, and I was onboard until I was discharged to report to the Naval reserve in February 1969. My actual expiration date from active duty was July but all those having six months or less left in their enlistment were discharge as the ship was headed back to Vietnam on its annual tour.

During the time I was on board we made yearly tours to Vietnam and would spend as much as nine months at a time out at sea in the western pacific.

It all started in August 1964, 3 months after I reported on board when we started conducting air strikes over North Vietnam, we would be stationed on the Gulf of Tonkin in the South China Sea off the cost of Viet Nam. Our station was called "Yankee Station". This is where we would spend up to 9 months in that area with short R&R (rest and recreation) visitations to nearby ports.

As I mentioned before I first reported aboard the ship in May 1964 after serving ten months of duty in Hawaii. In early 1966 I was promoted to 3rd class Boatswain's Mate (E-4). Besides other various duties, one of my duties was standing 4-hour long duty or watch as we called it. My watch was up on the bridge of the ship. This is the area where the captain is at along with other officers. The ships command and control is located here, to include the steering of the ship which include the helmsman or person that drives the ship, the person that controls the engines, and the person with a head set to communicate with certain key personnel and a messenger. All of these are enlisted men. The officers normally there besides the captain are the operations officer, navigator officer (OOD) and Officer of the Deck and the (JOOD) Junior Officer of the Deck. During normal hours there can also be more people around such as the Marine who serves as a bodyguard (orderly) to the captain and other officers.

The ships' Captain of course is usually there to oversee all of the ships operations and make all final decisions and give orders. From this location one can see the whole ship's flight deck and all the personnel moving about. An almost complete 360° view of the ocean around the ship is visible from this area.

Along with the persons that I mention there is an enlistee called a Plotter. This plotter has a huge plastic screen in front of him and keeps track of every ship in the area as well as every aircraft up in the air.

Under this deck (level) there is another section where you have flight control. These are the people who control flight operations, radar, and other needed ships functions, and although these persons are physical somewhere else on the ship, they all report to the main bridge.

And there is one other very important person on the main bridge and that is the Boatswain Mate of the watch who is in charge of the enlistees. That was what I did when promoted and I was known as the Boatswain Mate of the watch. But before I went up in rank and became a petty officer, I had to qualify on various other functions to stand watch up on the bridge, such as being able to qualify as a helmsman (steering the ship) as well as to run the engines and the communication radios. All of these jobs required strict attention and the following of orders from the officer of the deck.

As Boatswain Mate of the watch, I was the senior enlistee in charge of all enlisted personnel at the bridge, was qualified in all functions that the enlisted men do and was in charge of training. Another function I did was that of giving instructions by means of the ships communicated system known as the 1MC to all the ship's crew. I would relay messages to all Hands by use of these means. When instructed by the OOD or JR-OOD the Boatswains Mate will inform all hands through this system, routine, and emergency.

The 1MC is a box attached to the bulkhead(wall) behind the steering section and the Boatswains Mate usually stands beside it, although he is permitted to wonder around as the other enlistees are not.

Anyway, to communicate the first thing that is done to obtain the attention of all hands is that the BM (Boatswains mate) blows (called piping) through a pipe (known as the BM's pipe) which he carries hanging on his chest with a lanyard. The BM then passes the word (as it's called). It will sound something like this. (Sound from the pipe) "Attention all hands, attention all hands" and then the message. The Boatswain Mate is directly responsible to the Officer of the deck.

One night while out in the south china sea I had been assigned to the watch during the off-flight hours and it was around two or three o'clock in the morning. I had the 12 to 4 am watch. There were no flight operations going on at the time and it was all quite up on the bridge and all one could hear was the humming of some of the instruments. Every time we were on Zulu station, the only visible lights that were allowed were small red lights. No white light could be visible anywhere outside of the ship. Due to this it was dark on the bridge, but one could see pretty well once your eyesight got adjusted to the dark.

This one night the silence was broken when all of a sudden, the plotter calls out "sir, unidentified bogey ", the officer of the deck yells out "aircraft?" "Negative sir, surface "the plotter replies. "Range? "The officer of the deck inquires "110 knots sir" (I'm using it as an example as I can't recall the exact knots) (1 knot equals to 1.150 miles) "bearing?" the officer inquires again. "Bearing two-five-zero sir," (again using an example) Speed? the officer inquires again "90 knots sir" (I am not sure of the speed as I wasn't paying much attention at the time but that what is sounded like) answers the plotter," WHAT?" says the officer who runs over to where the plotter is at. A conversation then takes place between the officer of the deck, the plotter, and the junior officer of the deck as all converge up to where the plotter was at with the chart. I was across the other side of the bridge at the time and couldn't hear the conversation except when they raised their voices. I could hear them saying" no, it can't be, must be a mistake" "call the Maddox and Turner Joy, and get confirmation, check to see if they have the bogey" yells the JOOD.

(These were our two Destroyers known as DD's which were always close by and served as our escorts) After a brief time and constant repeating of new bearings, range, and speed which seem to indicate that whatever it was, it was headed in our direction, and it was moving at an unbelievable speed.

The Officer of the deck tells me to call the captain. The captain slept and had his quarters right next to the bridge and there was always a Marine by his door serving as a guard. I told the Marine that the captain was needed at the bridge, and he took care of calling the captain. A few minutes later the captain walks into the bridge and there was a bunch of communications going on as they were briefing the captain as to what had taken place. The officer of the deck then asked the captain if he should scramble. (We always had two jets on standby and ready to lunge in case they were needed with the pilots in the planes and ready to go.)

Yes, says the captain, scramble. Bells start ringing, orders being yelled out, people start running on the flight deck. At the same time the OOD tells the JOOD "Bring it around to the wind." The JOOD yells at the Helmsman, "Helmsman, bring it right smartly to two nine zero ". The helmsman acknowledges in a loud voice "right smartly to two nine zero, aye aye sir" As the ship was turning the jet engines fired up and within two to three minutes the jets start ramming up, fire coming out of the rear engines and away they went. As the jets left the front of the ship all you could see was the afterburners lighting up the dark sky in front of us.

I went to my station next to he 1MC waiting, I felt any minute I would be told to call GQ (General Quarters) to the ship's crew, and I wanted to be ready.

By the Captain's chair there are some loudspeakers, and the captain is able to hear the conversations between the pilots and flight control and the captain is also capable of speaking to the pilots if he so desires. A few minutes later you could hear the conversations between the pilots as they were headed to intercept the bogey.

The planes were getting close enough to where they could get a visual when all of a sudden, the plotter yells out "We lost the bogey sir, it's gone" Whatever it was, it just disappeared. The pilots were also talking that they too had had a drop from radar. There was a lot of talking and discussions up in the bridge for about a half an hour and the two planes that were sent up checked the whole area and came back without finding anything. Finally, the planes returned and landed safely.

Of what I could gather from the conversations, the situation was puzzling because everything indicated it was a surface vehicle. However, there was no known surface vehicle capable of going that fast.

Yet, it could not be a plane because it was too low to the water. Either way, whatever it was, it was gone.

While discussing this with some shipmates I later learned from other Boatswains mates that these type of incident was not rare that similar things happened all the time.

THE LADY IN THE RED DRESS

After being discharged from the Navy I came home and had a challenging time finding a job right away. I had to settle for a job in the clothing manufacturing for minimum wage. My father-in-law who worked in construction invited me to go to Chicago with him and he assured me I would be making three times more then what I was now making. I had already applied for the police department, but the process was lengthy and since I had to wait, I decided this was a good opportunity to make some money while I waited.

My father-in-law was a drywall taper, and I was simply going to be a labor since I didn't know the job. Once there the job was already waiting for us as my father -in -law had already made all the arrangements. There were a couple of other men who served as labors and helpers and we would help out with whatever was needed and did most of the odd jobs, such as cleaning and making sure plenty of material was at hand and so on.

About a month after arriving, we were working on a five-story apartment building which was being build and was still lacking windows and doors. The neighborhood was a residential area and some large picture windows on the building faced the street. There was only one stairway leading up to the apartments on the side of the building, which was actually the fire escape. The elevators were not installed yet. We were working on the third floor where the drywall sheetrock had just been installed and while my father-in-law and his friend Fidel were taping the bedrooms another worker named Felipe and I were covering nails in the living room area which faced the street. My father-in-law and Fidel had a radio which was going full blast and they were singing and laughing as they worked.

It was close to noon time when I happen to look out the glassless window towards the street and saw what appeared to be a young woman with shoulder length brown hair wearing a red dress and high heels walking on the sidewalk. The dress was the type that was worn in the 50's and 60's by girls with petticoats. The third floor was about thirty feet above the sidewalk, and I was unable to see the young woman's face, I say young lady because the way she walked and her body figure she seemed to be young and had a pretty good shape, if I may say so.

I called to Felipe and motioned to him to look down at the sidewalk. We hardly ever saw any people walking around so outside of that fact, plus the fact that she seemed to be a knockout and the way men are, we both stood at the window hole looking down gawking.

The young woman made a right turn walking towards the stairway of our building, and again, due to the height I couldn't see her face, only the top of her head. She kept walking and disappeared around the side of the building as if about to climb up the stairway. Felipe and I stood there for a moment wondering if she was actually going to come up the stairway. The thought did enter that maybe she was an executive and had something to do with the apartments or she was a possible tenant who was checking out the progress of the apartments. Either way we kept our eyes glued to the entry area from the stairway to see if she came in.

A few minutes later to our great surprise and bewilderment we saw the young lady walk right into the apartment we were working in. She came in through the main entrance door (which had no door) to the apartment which lead to the living room area where Felipe and I were. She was about twenty feet from us but as she came in, she turned left into a hall that lead to where my father-in-law and Fidel were working without me being able to get a good look at her face, only a slight view of her side. It was a very a quick glance as the woman came in fast as if knowing precisely where she was going. As she went into the bedroom area where my father-in-law was working, Felipe and I quickly walked in that direction thinking that she was going to tell something to my father-in-law and Fidel, and we wanted a pretext to be there.

As we went into the bedroom following the same path, she had taken but having lost sight of her temporarily due to our hesitation, we saw my father-in-law and Fidel standing there with their mouths open and tools hanging from their hands on their side looking staring into one of the closets. They looked at us as we came in and said, "did you see that" (in Spanish). The lady in the red dress had walked into a closet and disappeared.

Needless to say, for the remainder of that day all we talked about was that woman in the red dress who walked up the stairway, came into our apartment and disappeared into the closet. All four of us saw it and after telling the story to my wife she would only say" what were you guys thinking about?" Nothing, of course, after all, I was with her father, I would never misbehave or have those type of thoughts.

STORY 30

THE PLAYFUL LITTLE GHOST

My son in law Albert became principal for Beall Elementary located in the central part of El Paso in 2003. Beall School is one of the oldest schools in El Paso and is located in what is considered as a low-income area. The population there is prominent Hispanic (Mexican), and many are new immigrants.

Albert told me that one day after the school had closed, he was making his rounds checking the halls and classrooms before going home to make sure no one was left behind and all was secure. Albert would usually shake doors and make sure those that were supposed to be locked where locked and at the same time make sure no one was still left in the building.

Albert says he came upon a restroom that the door would not open. It was a boy's restroom and these restrooms for the children's safety could not be locked. The only way to lock it was on the very top (on the outside) where a child could not reach. Albert noticed that the lock on the top was not engaged but even then, he couldn't open the door. After trying without success for a while Albert called the school janitor (who lived on the grounds) to come over and assist thinking somehow the door had become jammed and needed some tools to repair it.

Juan the resident janitor came over and also tried opening the door without any success. They tried opening the door by turning the key on the top on and off, and even thought the door was unlocked they still couldn't open it. It seemed as if something was blocking the door from the inside. Albert explained to the janitor that he had tried pushing on the door with his shoulder (Albert is 6'5") thinking that it might have been stuck but the door didn't give.

After trying for a while, the janitor said" oh, I know what it is" Juan then leaned on the door and started talking softly towards the inside saying "Come on little ghost, please open the door for us, and go play somewhere else, please little Ghost, be nice" Juan repeated this a couple of times then he simply put the key on the top lock and upon turning the key the door opened.

Albert didn't know what to think or say. The Janitor who had been working at Beall for about forty-five years explained to Albert that this was somewhat common. Juan explained that small children haunted the school. At night children's voices could be heard on the halls as they ran and laughed.

There were many teachers who would not stay alone late because, they too had heard strange sounds. Juan had heard these noises ever since he started working there and wasn't afraid. He had since learned to talk to the ghost, and they would usually do as told. They were not aggressive or mean, they were simply children playing.

For the remainder of his time at Beall school Albert didn't have any trouble anymore, but of course he now knew that all he had to do was to ask nicely.

THE LITTLE INDIAN IN THE CLASSROOM

In the spring of 2015, my son-in-law Albert was made the first principal at the newly build Herrera Elementary in El Paso located on the west part of El Paso. Albert would later relate the following story to me.

Albert said that one day the school nurse and a fifth-grade teacher had taken a 5th grade student to him with the following story. The teacher related that during a class period while all the children were quietly doing their class assignment one of the boys walked up to her and said" teacher, there is a boy in the class that shouldn't be here and he's bothering me" The teacher looked up and scanned the room and not seeing anything unusual told the boy "Where?" and the boy said "over there at the corner" not turning around the boy simply motioned with his eyes and lifted his arm and pointed with his hand still having his back towards the classroom. The teacher again looked towards the corner and didn't see anything. At this moment the teacher felt that the boy was playing a joke, but this boy was not a disciplinary type of boy,the boy was usually a good student, never got in trouble and seeing how serious his face was she asked " and how does he look like?" and the boy replied, "his an Indian." "And what is he wearing?" the teacher asked looking towards the back corner of the classroom "nothing, just the cloth covering his private parts."

For a second the teacher didn't know what to think or do and in order not to disrupt the classroom and since some of the students were now looking at them wondering what was going on, she asked the boy to go with her to the hall. Once in the hall the teacher got one of her neighboring teachers to come out to the hall and she briefly told the other teacher of what was going on and they both interrogated the boy further and learned that the boy claimed that the Indian boy had been following him around for some time. The Indian boy was even at his home and his bedroom and would not let him do things, and that he never spoke, just stared at him all the time. When asked if he knew what the Indian boy wanted, he said he didn't know. Both teachers were puzzled and decide to take the boy to the nurse.

Again, the boy goes through his story with the nurse who sees that the boy is serious very serious as he tells her about the little Indian. The nurse knowing the boy, knew that he had never shown any type of mental problems and wonders if these are not hallucinations, but at the same time, it was obvious the boy was suffering from some type of mental problem.

The nurse felt it best to have the principal be informed, with the recommendations that the child receive some type of mental evaluation. It was then that the child was taken to Albert who was told all that had happened.

After hearing the story, Albert called the boy's parents who after being informed didn't seem too concern and said that they had already taken him to a doctor a few times in the past, but that there were other family members who also saw things like that and that they would eventually go away.

Albert didn't know what to do next but being that the boy was not violent, didn't seem to disturb anyone and his parents were fully aware he decided to let it go at that, and just monitor the situation.

I asked Albert a few months later about the boy and he said he was still going to school and that he hadn't said anything anymore. But it was something his family knew and were aware of so there was not much more he could do.

THE ANGEL IN
THE BACKYARD

Lorena (Lory) my daughter told me this story that she witnessed in 1996 shortly after giving birth to her son Albert III. Lory tells me that one day around ten or eleven o'clock in the morning as she went about her daily shores and as she passed by the back-yard window, for some unknown reason she looked outside. To her amazement as she looked outside, she saw a person passing by the window only about three feet away from her. Due to the windows visibility, she was only able to see the person for a brief time as it passed in front of the window, and she thought she saw something but was unsure if in fact it was what she thought it was.

So, in order to confirm what she thought she saw, she went up to the window and leaned on it to look outside and get a better look and although she was restricted of the view, she was still able to see enough to see what it was. She describes the figure as an Angel.

Lory says that even though she didn't get full details and it was only for a few seconds she was able to see enough that she knew it was tall figure and it was completely white. It had long white hair, a long white robe type garment, big white wings which were about two feet taller than the person and came down past his waist. Lory says that she had no doubt that is was an angel and she describes it as a male in its mid-twenties with perfect facial features and walked in a slow and down motion looking straight ahead as he walked from her left to her right till, she lost sight due to the angle.

Lory was alone at the house at the time and just stood there trying to see where the Angel had gone but was unable to see it. Lory says she felt no fear at the time and was only surprised and in wonder. The backyard is completely fenced in, and no one can get in and it is difficult to jump over.

Lory never saw that Angel again but has never forgotten it and on occasions Lory will look out the window in hopes that she might see that Angel again.

It was a beautiful and peaceful experience, Lory says.

THE FREEZING BEDROOM

The following story took place in my own home. Marco my son was in his early teens when this occurred to him. Marco was hesitant on telling his story because he says that every time, he tells it, it's like reliving it all over again. It was a long time before I heard of it.

Marco recalls that he was walking down the hall from his bedroom and as he turned the corner, he felt someone, or something pull him from the back. It was a powerful force pulling on him and he couldn't free himself from it. The force pulled him into his bedroom and into a papasan chair he had in his bedroom. Marco recalls fighting and trying to get away from this force that held him down on the chair and the struggle was so furious that it caused the chair to tip from side to side as he tried to free himself.

Just then Marco recalls wakening up and realizing it was just a bad dream. But for some reason Marco found himself standing in the middle of the dark and cold bedroom. Marco recalls that his bedroom was so cold that he was shivering, and he could see the breath coming out of his mouth. There was also a strange feeling as if someone was in the room and Marco lay down in his bed to cover himself up with the blankets.

Again, Marco felt as if he was awakening from a dream and this time, he was under the covers shivering from the cold and feeling his breath under the blankets as it was really cold. Marco was afraid and he could feel as if there was someone over him. The presence of someone there was so strong that Marco started to pray as he pulled the blankets up over his head. Marco closed his eyes and prayed that the cold and the horrific experience he was having would go away. Marco just kept praying over and over again not wanting to feel or think of anything and concentrating heavily on his praying.

Marco doesn't know how long this went on throughout the night, but it seemed forever, and it seemed that eventually somehow, he must have fallen asleep.

In the morning Marco got up and felt very tired as if had gotten very little sleep. As he prepared himself to go to school Marco thought about the incident during the night and realized that it had all been a very bad dream, but yet it all seemed so real.

Upon his return from school that day and upon going into his bedroom he noticed that the bottom portion of the papasan was broken. Something he hadn't noticed before he went to school.

Marco had previously hanged on the wall of his bedroom some devil horns and a pitchfork he had bought a few days before. Marco says that he had bought these horns which he had seen for sale because he thought they were cool. These were the same type of horns that a leader of a devil worshipers group used. Marco bought them thinking it would be fun to put them on for Halloween.

However, his mother did not like them and had told Marco repeatedly to get rid of them. Of course, Marco simply laughed at his mother and kept the horns on the wall.

But now, seeing them there on the wall, and after what had happened the previous night Marco had second thoughts and decided to remove the devil horns and fork down and he threw them away.

Never again did Marco experience anything like that the remainder of the years he slept in that bedroom.

Marco always wondered what had happened that night as although he felt it was a dream, he was sure he was awake for part of it, it was so real. He didn't know if he was dreaming that he was dreaming but still awake or if he was awake thinking he was dreaming.

And he could never explain how the papasan got broken being that it was such a sturdy piece of furniture.

THE LITTLE GHOST
IN THE BED

In the late 1970's my father-in-law, Alejandro started to build his house in Socorro Texas. His house was right behind my parent's house on the back street. My father had an acre of land while my father-in-law had half an acre which I had sold to him.

Soon after completing the house my father-in-law, his wife Socorro, son Ludovico and daughter Leticia moved in from Juarez Chihuahua Mexico where they had been living for many years.

My father-in-law and my mother-in-law would frequently make trips to Chihuahua to visit relatives and in the process would leave their children who were in their late teens by themselves. So, the kids were accustomed to frequently being by themselves.

A few years later Ludovico got married and moved out of the house leaving Lety as the only other occupant besides my in laws. Whenever possible I would allow my daughter Lory to spend a few days with Lety so she wouldn't be by herself. Lory and Lety were 8 years apart but got along very well.

There were always stories that the girls would tell, like someone turning on the T.V. or turning the lights on and off and everyone would simply laugh at them and ignore them thinking it was just a suggestive thing of the girls who were naturally afraid of being by themselves. My in-laws would simply tell them that "Es Mike "or "Es Marco."

Marco and Mike were two brothers of my wife who passed away when still very young. I never knew Mike but when I got married, I did know Marco. There was some type of hereditary illness that caused the male children of my mother in laws family that kept the children from growing in size and they would constantly be ill and eventually die. None of them would reach adulthood. Marco died when he was 9 years old and was about the size of a 6-year-old. He was very smart and a practical joker. The illness would not affect their minds at all and were normal in every way except that they were smaller than other kids of their own age. We named my son after him after he was born.

Lety says that she had the habit of every morning when she woke up, she would always walk down the hall to my in-law's bedroom. Since Lety didn't have a window in her bedroom with good visibility, she would simply walk into my in laws bedroom say hi to them and look outside the window towards the back yard and she would stretch. She would say good morning to the world and after a few minutes she would get ready for school.

Lety says that on one of these occasions when she was by herself, she got up as usual,went to the bedroom of my in law's, looked out the window and after stretching, for some unknown reason, she looked towards my in-law's bed and saw a small transparent figure of a child laying in the bed.

The size of the figure was of about a 3- or 4-year-old child who was lying on the bed. The transparent figure had no distinguishable features; it was only like the outline of a gelatinous like type of transparent material. The figure sat up, turned to where the feet were hanging over the bed, stood up and disappeared. However, the compression on the bed was still there and it lasted for a while.

Lety says that she really didn't feel scared, it was more of a surprise and wonderment if she had really seen something or not.

After if few minutes of just standing there in amazement she walked away and started to dress.

She never saw that figure again and for a long time didn't mention it to anyone. Various things happened in that house throughout the years and many of them to Lety.

STORY 35

THE MEAN SPIRIT

Lety my sister-in-law tells another story that also occurred at the home in Socorro.

Lety had her appendix removed in her early twenties by her brother who is a surgeon in Juárez Mexico. After the operation and once Lety was stable enough to travel, she was brought back to El Paso by her parents to recover at home. Once home she was placed in her bedroom to recover.

Lety's bedroom was located next to her parents and her mother had made her as comfortable as she could and made sure Lety didn't need anything. Lety says that once her parents had set her up to rest and recover, her parents left her alone in her bedroom. It hadn't been long after they left when she had a strange, evil thing happened.

She hadn't been in her room long when she felt as if someone was pushing down against her fresh wound where she had been operated on. The pain was unbearable, and she bends forward to ease the pain. The entity (for a better word) kept pushing down and Lety was hurting. Lety recalls thinking it felt as if there was an actual person that was pushing down on her side.

Lety also recalls telling the entity "Please don't, please it hurts, please leave me alone, go away, please" but the entity seemed to only

113

push harder "please leave me alone, why are you bothering me, go away " Lety would say.

All the time Lety kept trying to yell and scream to get her parents attention to get some help, but no sound would come out her mouth. Lety would put her hands over her wound to protect the area and to keep the entity from pushing, but it didn't help much.

Finally, after gathering all her strength, and trying over and over again, Lety let out a big yell "MAMA, MAMA" she yelled.

Both her parents came running to her room and as soon as her parents entered the room the thing stopped. Lety was in tears and moaning from the pain. She quickly told her mother and father what had occurred, and her mother sat next to her and started to pray.

The entity did not bother her anymore.

STORY 36

THE SWINGING ROSARY

Lety also mentions this story about her mother when she was gravely ill in bed and the doctors prognoses wasn't good, my mother-in-law wasn't expected to live long. Lety's mother (my mother -in-law) was named Socorro and she was a beautiful person in and out.

I have heard many jokes and man talking negatively about their mother in laws, but let me tell you, mine must have been the exception. As I said, my mother-in-law was a beautiful person, not only with me but with everyone she ever met.

She had suffered tremendously as a young woman having many of her children die very young after years of sickness. She spend her youth caring for sick children. For years she would nurse them only to have them die in their pre-teens. That was one of the reasons why she was so kind and loving and although someone else might have felt abandoned by God and would have held a grudge against God, she never did.

Anyway, Socorrito (as we lovingly called her) became ill and for a couple of years it was touch and go until one day she became bed ridden. Due to her condition Medicare supplied a person to go to the house every day and cook meals, clean house, and help out Socorrito and her elderly husband.

The lady who took care of my in laws' was named Olga and

Olga was a Christian belonging to a newly started Christian sect faith church.

One day Olga asked Lety if she would mind if her Pastor would come and pray with Socorrito. At first Lety refused, stalling, and telling Olga she would think about it. Lety was the only other person living at the time with my in laws and took charge their care.

Lety knew that her mother had always been a very devoted Catholic and didn't much care for the other religions and their beliefs. But after Olga kept insisting and asking so many times Lety asked her father of what he thought. Her father felt no harm could come from it and agreed. So, it was agreed, and a date and time was set.

On the wall above Socorrito's head, and above her bed was a statue of El *Nino de Atocha,* which was one of Socorrito's favorite Saints (see previous stories). Over the statue of El Niño, was Socorrito's rosary which was hanging from the wall. Socorrito at this stage was unconscious most of time or sleeping. All her life Socorrito had been a very faithful and devoted Roman Catholic.

The previously mention Pastor and his wife arrived just before noon one day and his wife was also a pastor. Olga introduced them to Lety and my father-in-law and shortly after were told where Socorrito's bedroom was at, and Lety accompanied by her father escorted them. At the foot of the Socorrito's bed, the Pastor, his wife, Olga, Lety, and her father kneeled down.

The pastor took out his bible and started to read. A few minutes into the pastor reading Lety noticed the rosary over the saint was starting to move as it slowly started to swing gradually from side to side. The more the pastor would read the more the rosary would swing.

It was so obvious that everyone noticed it, but no one would say anything. After a few minutes the pastor simply said" we better go" They stood up and walked out of the house in a quick pace without saying much more.

After the Pastor and his wife left Lety, her father and Olga were very silent as if no one wanted to mention what they had seen.

All three of them knew what they had witnessed, but it was as if nobody wanted to recall it and were still in a semi shock condition.

Needless to say, they were never invited again, and Olga never mentioned them again.

A few months later Mami Socorrito passed away.

STORY 37

THE BABY STROLLER

My older sister Guadalupe told to me this story. It's something that happened while I was away doing my military service in the 1960's.

My mother for many years had a lady that would help her around the house with housework. My mother was getting up there in age and had difficulty doing certain type of housework.

This lady's name was Chonita, and she went to my parents' house in a weekly basis to help my mom with cleaning, ironing, and other general housework.

Through the years Chonita and my mom had become good friends.

Chonita lived in what is named the second ward section of El Paso which is the southern portion of downtown El Paso next to the Rio Grande that separate the U.S. from Mexico. This was a low-income area. Not to say that our area was any better, but many of the people living in the 2nd ward were newly arrived immigrants.

Also living in the 2nd ward was an ex-wife of my granduncle Pete Araiza. Her name was Luz, and she was an Asian lady who was up on years and had maintained a close relationship with mom after Uncle Pete had passed away. Not that they frequented each other but they would on occasions stop and talk whenever their paths crossed.

Mom had introduced Luz and Chonita one day and since they

both lived in the 2nd ward, not far from each other they had become friends.

One day while Chonita was at my mom house, she mentioned to my mom that one of Luz's daughters had just had a baby and was having a tough time as she was not financially stable and was lacking a lot of baby items among other things. Mom recalled that she had a baby stroller that wasn't being used anymore and asked Chonita if she would take the stroller and some other items to Luz so she could give it to her daughter since it wasn't needed anymore and maybe she could use it. Chonita said she would be happy to do it and she took it with her.

About a month went by and Mom forgot all about it. One day while downtown Mom went to the Rainbow bread store to buy some bread and on her way in, she came across Luz who was also there. After a friendly greeting Luz thanked my mom for the baby items and the stroller. They exchanged greetings and after a brief conversation departed on their own ways.

That following week when Chonita came to my moms' house to clean, Mom mentioned to Chonita that she had come across Luz a few days ago at the Rainbow store and that she had thanked her for the stroller and that Luz looked really good.

Chonita with a strange look looked at my mom and said, "You know that Luz died, don't you" No! my mom says, oh God, when did she die? asked my mom. Chonita said over 2 weeks ago. No! mom said, it can't be I just saw her a couple of days ago. When did you say she pass? Chonita repeated 2 weeks ago, and they buried her a couple of days later.

Oh my God, mom would say I can't believe this, are you sure?

Mom kept repeating that as they both checked the days on the calendar to conform the dates and sure enough Luz had died a week and a half before my mom saw her at the store.

STORY 38

THE FLYING ALTAR BOY

Albert Reyes (Senior) my son-in-law's father told me this story which took place in the late 1940's.

It happened when he was growing up in Durango, Mexico in his grandmother's house. Albert's maternal grandmother was raising Albert and his brother at the time and Albert thinks he was about three years old.

Albert recalls that he and his brother were constantly fighting, and his grandmother would lock Albert in a small dark room as punishment. The house they were living in did not actually belong to his grandmother, it was a house she was renting.

According to neighbors the house had at one time belonged to a man who had been hanged right outside the house by some men during the Mexican revolution. The actual reason for his hanging was not known, but many rumors circulated and one of these rumor was that the man who had previously owned the house was well off and was known to have had a sizeable amount of money. It was unknown if the people who hanged him hanged him for his money or something else having to do with the unrest in Mexico at the time. Either way it was believed that if the murders had taken some money, it was not all of it.

It was believed that this man had hidden the greatest majority of money somewhere around the house. Of course, during these years there were no banks and if there were, people would not use them.

Most people would hide whatever cash they had which usually consisted of gold or silver coins as paper money had no real value. People would use various non suspected locations throughout the promises to hide the coins. Some people in this case suspected that the money was hidden in the water well. Another story was that the revolutionists had come looking for the money and when the man refused to tell them where he had hidden it, they hanged him. But nobody knew for sure.

Albert goes on to say that on various occasions when he was locked inside the dark adobe room for fighting, he was able to look underneath an opening on the bottom of the door and could see under the bed a bunch of lit candles. He would back himself against the wall and just stare at the candles as they flickered.

Albert who at the time had a problems with stuttering would tell his grandmother of what he had seen as best as he could referring to the candles, but nothing was ever done, his grandmother would just acknowledge him and that was it and either didn't believe him or simply didn't care.

But the strangest thing which not only he had observed but other people in the house as well was the flying altar boy. Albert says that it was actually a figure which was dressed in red and white just like altar boys dressed but that it had no head. Thinking back now Albert thinks that maybe it was just the clothing.

The figure would fly around the room in a triangle pattern over and over again. Albert says that in more than one occasion there were more than one person in the room who saw it but all that could be done was just stand there in shock and observe the figure fly around until it disappeared.

Of course, no one would talk about what they saw they just hoped it didn't appear again, but it usually did. Albert recalls seen this flying person, clothes or whatever more than once and what he learned to do was just try and ignore it as there was nothing anyone could do about it. It usually didn't last long, and it could occur at any time.

In time Albert grew up and he and his brother moved away. But Albert says he never forgot what he had seen when living with his grandmother.

Albert says he always wondered why nobody would talk about it as everyone living there or who visited regularly knew of the incidents that occurred. People just went about as if nothing and he learned to do the same thing.

STORY 39

BURIED AGAINST HIS WILL

Isela one of my wife's childhood friends told me this story in the summer of 2014.

Isela who was born and raised in Mexico and lived most of her life there and in the early 1970's married a man from Mexico DF. Her husband, Raul worked for the Mexican Federal government in law enforcement as a federal agents assistant and was from a prominent Mexican family. His brother also worked for the federal government and the whole family was well known among the federal politicians in Mexico.

Raul's mother was one of those ladies who ran her household with an iron fist. Her children always did everything to please her and would seldom go against her wishes. There were always servants around the house.

To be able to promote to a full federal Agent withing the Mexican federal Police, one must serve a certain time as an assistant to a full pledge agent. Within time and depending on the job the individual does and with recommendations he could be promoted to Full Agent.

Raul always wanted to work within this field and was soon working as an assistant. Of course, if that person had any type influence, he won't be working as an assistant long and that was the case with Raul. Raul was soon promoted and became a Full Federal Police officer.

His job within the force would require frequent traveling and moving within the Republic of Mexico with different assignments. Once married Isela would usually accompany him on his new assignments. They were never in one place too long. But whenever they came to Juarez, which was Isela's hometown, Raul would always say he loved this city.

Raul loved Juarez so much he told Isela that when he died, he wanted to be buried there. Jokingly Isela would tell him "Put it in writing, you know how your mother is?"

The years passed and they had two little girls and the traveling for Isela was not as easy anymore having to care for the children but would do so whenever possible. Isela stayed in Juarez temporarily and started a home.

Raul came to Juarez frequently and he would always say "Oh I love this place, remember Isela I want to be buried here."

At the age of forty-seven while stationed in Nuevo Laredo Mexico (the whole family was living there) Raul died in his sleep one night. The reason was never known (authors note ; or Isela would not reveal it) Isela got a hold of the federal Attorney General's office for whom Raul worked for and in no time the squad commander was at Isela house helping her with all the arrangements. Of course, Raul's parents in Mexico City were also informed.

In a couple of days, the Federal Attorney General's Office owned airplane came in from Mexico City to pick up the body. Isela says that it was a large old airplane that was regularly used to transport personnel. Isela was asked by the Commandant where she wanted the body to be taken to and she replied to Juarez. The Commandant said he would make arrangements and later came back saying that the word had come down from Mexico City to take the body to Mexico City. Isela refused to accept that and questioned who it was that did not want to comply with her wish. She told the commander that it had been her husband's wish.

The reply soon came, and it happened that Raul's mother wanted the body taken to Mexico City.

A few days went by as communications went back and forth and finally the commander told Isela that he was sorry, but the body had to be taken to Mexico City that those were the orders from his superiors.

Isela then felt that she didn't have the time nor political power to fight Raul's family and win, so she went along with it.

Soon the body was brought into the plane and besides Isela and the commander only the pilot and copilot were on the plane. The plane taxied down the runway and after going up made a circle and came back. The pilot said they were having some type of problems and they needed the plane checked. After a small delay they were off again, and again they had to come back. This happened three times and finally the plane was able to get going and they were on their way to Mexico City.

In Mexico City they took the body from the Funeral Home and placed it in a hearse. They were going to a small Chapel close to the cemetery. No sooner had they left the funeral home when the hearse broke down. After a few minutes of making mechanical repairs, they were on their way again, and again the hearse died out. After the second time they were able to make it to the Chapel.

After the services at the Chapel, they put the body in the hearse and this time they couldn't get the hearse started no matter what the mechanics did to it.

They finally put the coffin in a Suburban that was carrying the flowers.

Raul was laid to rest in a cemetery in Mexico City of his mother's choosing, but Isela knew it had been done against her husband's wishes and Isela feels that Raul tried even in death did everything he could to fight against his mother and that he had fought all the way to the cemetery. Those close to her made regular comments of the occurrences and what seemed to be Raul's refusal.

Raul's remains still rest there, but Isela says against his wishes.

STORY 40

THE FLYING SWEATER

In the summer of 2014, while camping with my family as we do every year in the Sacramento Mountains at the Mescalero Indian reservation, we were accompanied by the Hardin family who had joined us in their motorhome.

One night while sitting around the campfire as we did every night, my grandchildren asked me to tell them some scary stories. I took the opportunity to explain to the Hardin family that I was in the process of collecting scary and unexplainable stories for a book and asked them if they had ever experienced any unexplainable or scary events. The Hardin family was composed the mother Mayra, her husband and two teenage children.

To my surprise the Hardin's looked at each other and said "yes." Mayra who was actually my daughter's friend (they were both teachers at the same school) said that she had grown up in Juarez Mexico where not only her, but many of her family members heard and saw strange things. Mayra then told her son Ethan to tell me what he had seen when he was growing up at that house.

Ethan went on to say that when he was around nine years old, he and his cousin were playing hide and seek inside his grandmother's house and that he had run up the stairs to the second floor to hide inside a bedroom (which was his mother's bedroom) and he sat on the floor not wanting to make any noise.

Ethan than saw through the corner of his eye as if something had fall down to the floor from a standing ironing board. He turned around to see what it was, and it was a sweater. As he looked at the sweater on the floor the sweater started moving and floating up in the air. It went up as high as the ironing board.

The sweater danced around for a few seconds in the air then drooped to the floor again.

At this Ethan became scared and ran out of the room.

According to Mayra many other strange events happened in that house and many of the family members experienced them, but no one really seemed to talk about them at the time.

STORY 41

THE CRYING BABY

In July 2014 while celebrating my daughter's birthday at my house, I asked those present if any of them had ever experienced any paranormal type of activity. My uncle Lencho's granddaughter Maxie said she did. She said something strange happen to her once or twice and asked why.

I explained that I was collecting stories for a book that I wanted to publish. She replied that in fact she had some strange things that had happened to her, and she went on to tell me three stories but the one that really got to me and really hit home and goes like this.

Maxie said that one day she had gone to her grandparents' house (my uncle Lencho and Aunt Ceci) who lived by themselves and who for the same reason, she frequented often. On this one day she had fallen asleep on the floor as she was really tired. My Aunt Ceci who was also present at the party then interrupted and said that Maxie was snoring so loud that she decided to make a recording so that when she woke up, she could hear herself and see how loud she was snoring, otherwise she would never believe it. Ceci recorded Maxie for some time than put the phone away.

After Maxie woke up, Ceci laughingly told Maxie of how loud she was snoring and knowing that she would not believe it, told her she had recorded her and at the same time giving the recording to Maxie so that she could listen to it for herself.

Everyone came around and laughing stood by as the recording was turned on. After a couple of seconds of hearing Maxie snoring and while the recording was still active a child is heard on the tape crying.

This stunned everyone as they looked at each other in disbelieve of what they were hearing. There were no babies at the house. Maxie was already in her 30's. They listened to the tape over and over again and sure enough there was no mistaking that a child was heard crying in between Maxie snores.

I asked Maxie if she still had the recording and she said she did and started looking for it on her cell phone. After about 2 minutes searching through her phone, she said "I got it, you want to listen to it?" Of course, I said, and she suggested we go into a quiet room in the house, and I listened to it.

She turned the recording on and after about three snores and some heavy breathing all of a sudden you can clearly hear a baby cry for about two – three seconds. When I heard this, I got goose bumps on my arms. She said if I wanted to hear it again and I said "NO." It was weird and at the same time scary.

I told those present at the party of the recording and what it entailed and asked if they wanted to hear it, but nobody wanted to hear it once they knew what it entailed and how shaken I was

STORY 42

THE SKINNY HAND

During August 2014 my Goddaughter Veronica along with her husband and two small children came to visit us. During the visit I told her of the collection of stories I was collecting for a book and asked her if anything had ever happened to her or her husband Victor.

Victor stated he didn't believe in any of the supernatural things people talk about, but Veronica said she did have something that for a long time had been occurring to her.

Veronica went on to tell me that ever since she could remember she used to have a pain on her arm up towards the shoulder. That this pain even caused her fingers to go numb sometimes. She was taken various times to doctors and had had a series of examinations, but nothing was ever really found. She was told that it was probably nerve problems and outside of traditional treatment which never cured her, nothing was ever done. She learned to live with it.

Later on, somebody told Veronica about this lady that could possibly help her, and Veronica made an appointment to see this person. Veronica said that she arrived at a normal looking house but that once she stepped inside, she was astonished upon seeing all the candles and heavy presence of saint and angel figures and Veronica then realized she was in the company of a "curandera "(some people refer to them as white witches).

The lady was kind and attentive and after a lengthy interview the lady told Veronica that it could be something that had been passed on to her from one of her parents or grandparents. The lady said that sometimes people are harmed by spells and the effects and ailments continue with the following generations even after the original person is gone.

But, none the less the lady said she could cure her but that there was a possibility that she could start having some bad dreams. Veronica thought about it for a while then agreed.

Sure, enough shortly after staring treatment Veronica started having bad dreams which usually consisted of demon type creatures. Veronica told this to the lady who said that the bad dreams were often the evil spirits fighting back the cure.

Veronica kept her regular visits to this lady's house for about two months and the lady never charged her anything for her service. The only thing the lady asked for was repayment for two candles that she had given to Veronica which Veronica was to let burn completely to the base and then bring them back to her with all the melted wax.

During these two months the lady would put some cotton on Veronica shoulder and wet it down with holy water. The lady would then pull small strings of cotton very gently and Veronica says that she actually felt as if something was being pulled out from her shoulder.

Once the handles had melted, she took them back to the lady who examined the melted wax and said that often one can she faces, insects or other things in the melted wax which can identify the intruder or person who caused the harm. Veronica never knew what if any the lady found on the melted wax she took.

Veronica's shoulder did start to get better, and eventually she stopped going to see the lady, but she then stated having some unusual dreams or out of body type of experiences.

Veronica would also feel a tremendous sense of fear and felt a presence. She would often see everything around the room and see herself in bed and would have to start praying because the sense of fear was so great.

She also started to see some black smoke type balls flooding around the room going around and around. All of this would occur frequently and eventually she learned that she could wake herself up (although she seemed to be awake, she knew she was asleep) by breathing really hard and fast while praying. However, on one occasion while going through the ordeal she felt a hand on her shoulder and saw a long skinny hand, almost skeleton with long ugly nails grabbing her shoulder. These things happened often but not with any frequency, and she learned to deal with it and blame it all on anxiety attacks.

Years later and once she got married, she confined in her husband and told him everything that had been going on throughout her life. Of course, Victor listened and was compassionate about it, but he didn't believe on those things. Veronica continued to once in a while, even after getting married, to experience some of the ordeals. She however learned that once she was going through one of this things if she started to breathe hard enough Victor would hear her and wake her up. This helped her as a defensive mechanism.

After some time and on one of those nights that she had one of her experiences Victor surpassingly enough had the same type of dream that Veronica was having, Victor saw the same identical things but, Victor angrily told the entity to leave and leave his wife in peace and never come back.

Miraculously ever since then Veronica stopped having those dreams and hasn't had an experience of that nature since then.

However, in more the one occasion her children (she had a 2-year-old and a 3-year-old at time of interview) have cried at night and when she has gone over to see what was the matter, she has found them sitting up in bed looking around with a scared look in their face.

Veronica in these occasions has laid down in bed with them to help them go back to sleep and she has felt that presence and fear she used to feel but not as great.

Thank God she says, that is not often. At this time, she doesn't know what she will do if it continues with her children.

STORY 43

THE LITTLE FIREMAN

Veronica my godchild (see story 42) told me about an incident that happened to one of her coworkers.

Anna (her coworker) used to work with Veronica at Telcel in Chihuahua, Mexico in the early 2000's. Anna was not originally from the city of Chihuahua but had moved to Chihuahua and rented an apartment after obtaining employment with Telcel.

Veronica and Anna became good friends and on a couple of occasions she visited Anna at her apartment which was a large one room apartment which was divided into a small kitchen, dining area and bedroom.

One day Anna came to work and told the following story. Anna says that for about two straight nights in a roll someone would knock on her door around 2 or 3 o'clock in the morning. Of course, Anna didn't answer and whoever it was would eventually go away.

On the third night Anna was going to bed and turned off the light on her nightstand after she laid down on her bed to go to sleep. She said shortly afterwards she felt as if someone had sat down on her bed besides her and she felt a flash of fear and quickly tried reaching out to turn the light on and in the process due to the darkness and haste she knocked some stuff to the floor from the nightstand. She stumbled with her hands until she eventually found the switch and turned the light on and to her astonishment, she saw standing next to her bed besides her a small boy about 4 years old. The little boy was wearing some coverall's and he had a fireman's hat on but it was more of a plastic play hat.

For a second, they both stared at each other without saying a word. Anna Then quickly pulled the blanket over her head and started to pray and cry and shaking at the same time. After what seemed like hours of crying and praying, she must have fallen asleep without her actually knowing it.

Next thing she remembers was feeling the daylight sun rays coming into her apartment. She knew it was day, but it had seemed like only moments had gone by. She slowly turned around to see if anyone was still next to her bed and also glanced around the room and not seeing anyone she quickly got up and got dressed thinking that the previous night incident must have been a bad dream. Nevertheless, she couldn't get out of the room quick enough.

But yet, it seemed so real and there was some of her personal stuff on the floor by the nightstand she didn't remember putting there but at the moment it was not a concern she hurried to ger ready to leave and go to work.

At work Anna's coworkers all gave different opinions of what had happened and most assured her it was a nightmare. After work Anna returned to her apartment but this time with some friends from work as she was still afraid to go by herself. Anna had stated that she was not going to stay at that apartment anymore and only wanted to get some clothes.

When she opened the door to the apartment, she and her companions saw that the bed had been made (she didn't have time to make it up when she left) and as they walked around towards the dining area, she and her coworkers saw on the floor two plates with its utensils set up as you would for a formal dinner. Like when little girls are playing house and they set up the table.

Her companions didn't know what to think and just mumbled to themselves. Needless to say, Anna didn't live in that apartment anymore. And as for coworkers who said it had only been a dream, they were silent.

STORY 44

THE BABYSITTER

In August 2015 my daughter-in-law Irene called me to tell me the following story. She had just hung up the phone talking to her sister Daniela who lives in Nacozari, Sonora Mexico. Daniela lives there with her husband and two children. A six-year-old boy and a 3-year-old girl. They had bought the house where they now live 3 years earlier.

It was a 2-bedroom house when they bought it but as the children grew, they had built another room to where they were now able to accommodate each child into their own bedroom.

Irene said that her sister and husband had the bad habit of going out once in a while and leaving the children alone. In occasions Daniela had told Irene about some strange things happening. These so-called strange things that her sister mentioned never really amounted to anything and to a certain extent they really didn't even seem strange until now.

Daniela went on to say that on various occasions her son had told her to close the curtains on his bedroom window because the eyes on the window would stare at him from outside. Although Daniela did close the curtains, she thought it was a child imagination thing and didn't pay much attention to it.

However, one day the little boy let out a yell that sounded as if he was in a panic or hurt, the type of yell that alerted her to the point she ran over to see what was going on in haste. She found her son on the floor crying saying that he couldn't get up. "Why can't you get up?" Daniela asked. "The cockroach won't let me and it's laughing at me" the boy said. Daniela laughed and helped him up and all was dismissed as child's joke.

On a corner of the little girls bedroom Daniela had an old baby crib which she used as a storage for all the boys toys and little girl dolls. Many of the dolls were stuffed type dolls as well as some of the other toy. Most of them were those the children did not play with anymore. So many had accumulated throughout the years that the crib was now full.

As her little girl grew a little older, she would frequently tell her mom to please cover them at night because they would bother her and scare her. Of course, Daniela again felt it was a kid thing, as she didn't believe in any of that scary type of things.

On one occasion she did remember that her daughter was playing with a toy that she had never seen before, and she asked her "where did you get that from?" "That little boy gave it to me" she replied." What little boy?" Daniela asked "The one with the green shirt" she said pointing towards her bedroom. Daniela peeped into the room and didn't see anything, and she thought it was an imaginary friend like all kids have and just dismissed it.

But, on this particular day during the phone call, Daniela told Irene she was in the kids bedroom sitting on one of beds folding clothes when she saw something through the corner of her eye on the crib and glanced up to see what it was and for a split second, she saw what seemed to her to be like a white transparent sheet coming out of the toys crib and fly rapidly over to her bedroom through the door which was next to the crib.

Daniela said she couldn't really explain what it was, but it scared the hell out of her. She ran to the kitchen and got a candle, lit it, and started to pray.

All of a sudden, all the stories and things that the kids had been telling her for years came to her mind.

Oh, poor kids she said, what other things have they seen?

Irene asked her what she was going to do, and she said she didn't know. Maybe just have the house blessed with holy water.

It is unknown what happened after this and if it continued or not. The fact remained that now she believed her children and was more observant.

STORY 45

GRANDPA VISITS DIANITA

The son of my wife's cousin Luis told me this story involving his sister Diana and her daughter Dianita. Back in late 2000, their dad Alberto died in Cuauhtémoc, Chihuahua Mexico.

Diana who lives in Guadalajara, Jalisco Mexico came to Cuauhtémoc for the funeral by herself, leaving her small daughter back in Guadalajara with her daughters father. Her daughter Dianita was about 4 or 5 years old at the time.

After the funeral services Diana went back home and shortly after arriving went in the room where Dianita was playing. Diana felt she needed to explain to her daughter the reason for her absence.

She started explaining to Dianita's that grandpa had died. Dianita just said, "yes, I know." Diana did not make much of that answer and went on to seat in a chair next to Dianita to further explain. As she was seating down, Dianita yelled "Don't seat there mom!" Diana asked why not? Dianita answered, "Because grandpa is sitting there, don't you see I am playing with him?"

Diana quickly got to her feet looked at the chair but was unable to see anything. Diana felt it was best just to leave it alone, didn't say more, and left the room.

STORY 46

MILITARY MANEUVERS

In December 2021, my wife, Grandson Marco, and myself along with my great granddaughter were driving to San Antonio Texas for the Christmas holidays. My grandson Marco was driving and as we conversed the writing of this book came up. My grandson then tells me" Grandpa I have a story for you, you won't believe."

Marco had joined the Army in October of 2020 and had gone to basic training in Oklahoma. Marco told me that in November 2020 while in basic training his company was on a long march where they walked all day with full packs. As evening came, they got to their final destination for the day, and all were tired after miles of marching all day long.

However, before nightfall, they had to set up tents but luckily for them the cooks were waiting for them with tents and dinner. Once they were set up, they would grab their chow and sit around to eat before getting ready to turn in for the night.

As they were all gathered around eating in the dark, someone yelled out to the group "hey look" pointing towards the sky which was a beautiful night full of stars. My grandson Marco along with all the others (he said there were close to two hundred soldiers) then observed three lights up in the sky in a vertical line close to each other. They would blink and when they came back, they would be in a horizontal position. They would blink again and come back in a vertical position. They did this back and forth a few times then all of a sudden, they all took off in flight in a very unbelievable rate speed towards the darkness and beyond.

Everyone just made oh sounds as it disappeared in the dark sky and looked at each other in amazement and unbelievable event they had all just witnessed.

No one said much expect "Oh wow did you see that? ",even the officers witnessed the event, and they too were quite.

STORY 47

UNEXPLAINABLE PHOTO

They say that a picture is worth a thousand words. That, I believe that's true.

People who have experienced something out of the ordinary, something unexplainable always have a challenging time trying to convince people of what they saw or experienced. The only and best way to convince and make others believe is the person has visible prove. And often that means a photograph. But even with cell phones now in days the person is not always, or should I say, seldom are they prepared since these things happen unexpectedly and no one is prepared to do that.

Let's face it, how many of us go around camera ready waiting for something to happen? The last thing one is thinking about is taking a picture as it usually takes minutes, sometime longer, for a person to realize just what it was that they experienced.

Not only that, but most of these things also happen in a flash. Yet, there are occasions when this is possible as we will see on the following two pictures. Sometimes its not that the person is trying to get something on film, that person is unaware at the time of what is taking place. Not until later does this come into play.

The first picture is something that happened in Nacozari Sonora Mexico on July 27th, 2015. This picture was sent to me by my daughter- in- law Irene. Both per stepfather and brother-in-law work in the copper mine as most men do in Nacozari Mexico.

This men are aware of the dangers working in the mine and normally pray and commend themselves over to our holy lady before going to work and going into the mines.

On the morning of July 27th at approximately 6:45 am as workers were headed for the mine through a heavy fog. Each in their own way saying their private prayers in silence as they walked together this happened.

Something unusual was observed by the group as they walked together. One of the workers named Grijalva who had his cell phone on hand was able to snap a shot of the following image. All present saw it and commented on the image they saw. The image did not last long but those few seconds left the miners speechless.

Many believe they saw the image of the Virgin Mary, but you be the judge. 1st Mine photo.

COMPARE

The second photo is one which was taken by my daughter Lorena. Lorena and her husband and children where on the road one day and Lorena thought the view by the highway was so beautiful that she thought about taking a snapshot with her cell phone as it was a beautiful morning.

She took the cell phone photo through the windshield of their GMC as she was the passenger on the front seat. Once she took the picture and looked at it, to her surprise a rosary also appeared on the photo. There was no explanation of this as they had no rosary anywhere on the dash or windshield of the car.

One thing is for sure. There are many mysterious and unexplainable things that occur everyday to normal people throughout the world.

Many will usually tell someone close ; others will simply keep it to themselves.

Afterall, they too sometimes can't believe what they have experienced, so if they are not sure, how is someone else going to believe them?

EPILOGUE

You have to admit that this world is made of opposites. You have up and down, inside, and outside, night and day, cold and hot, good, and bad, and you can go on and on. So, if you believe in good you must also accept bad and vice versa.

In the case of supernatural and incidents of unbelievable situations you have some who will argue that they are simply things that are confusing at the moment and that people due to the stress or emotional state of being at the time come up with a quick solution without thinking it out. That most of these things have an explanation and that people simply jump to conclusions and let their imagination fly away. They have a logical explanation they claim.

Well, I guess that can be true in some cases like the one I'm going to mention below of something that occurred while I worked with the Police department.

I was working the greave yard shift (11pm to 7 am) in the lower valley of El Paso known as Yesleta. The area was composed of the most eastern limits of El Paso. The district actually covered everything south of I-10 to the international boundary (the Rio Grande River) and east of around Thomas Manor area to the city limits which was about one miles east of Loop 375.

I can't recall who my partner was but usually after 2am when bars closed everything was quiet and we concentrated in checking local business for break ins. We would normally drive the patrol car slowly and use the patrol car spotlights to shine on the buildings and for suspicious vehicles parked around them. If we suspected something we could get out of the car and check further.

On this particular night it was around 4 in the morning, and we were checking businesses around Zaragoza Street south of the present day Tigua Indian casino. About three hundred yards south of our area was a bar situated on the west side of Zaragoza Street and it stood alone. There were no other buildings around or close to it and it was surrounded by a large dirt area used for parking. It set about thirty feet of the road (Zaragoza) and across the street was the cemetery which had a Rockwall fence around it.

We heard an alarm go off and flowed the sound headed south towards the U.S. port of entry which was about half a mile away. We then realized the alarm was coming from the bar that I mentioned that stood alone. We drove up got out and found the back door open. We checked inside and found all the vending machines broken into and the bar area and office ransacked but no intruders. We noticed that entry had been made through the roof using the air conditioner air ducts.

We called our dispatcher and requested they contact the owners and also requested for ID and R (identification and record) now referred to as CSI (crime scene investigation) in order that they take evidence such as checking for latens prints and taking photos. We didn't carry any type of equipment to do that job ourselves. We then went outside and sat in the patrol car to wait and for my partner to start writing the report. Meanwhile I just set behind the steering wheel. The units windows were rolled down and it was very quiet morning, no traffic no people up yet.

After a few minutes I heard some noises which seemed to be coming from the cemetery. The Rockwall fence was only about forty feet from where our unit was parked. I turned to my partner and asked, "Did you hear that" and he said "yes." The noise had stopped so we just listened and sure enough a few minutes later we heard it again and it sounded like muffled voices or something similar to that. I said, "you hear that?" turning to look at him. "yes" he said as he raised his head up from writing the report. "Do you want to check it out?" He said, "No!" I said, do 'YOU" want to check it out?" "No, he said.

So, we just sat there, and it wasn't a constant noise in fact we only heard it once or twice and we couldn't quite identifiably the sounds coming from the cemetery. We each had our own ideas, and fears (for a better lack of words) but we didn't talk about it, and we didn't want to know anything about it. Soon they stopped for good, but it didn't completely leave our minds. I know we both kept thinking about it.

The owner showed up. We walked through the business with the owner making sure the crime scene was preserved and getting more information for our report and about an hour later the detective from ID&R showed up. He started taking photos and dusting items checking for latens. The owner stayed with the detective and my partner, and I walked out.

It was now getting clear outside and the first rays of sunshine were visible and soon the morning commuters would start filling the streets. My partner and I then decided to walk up to the cemetery to check the area where the sounds were coming from last night since we couldn't see in that direction in the dark. As we crossed the street approached the fence, we saw a beer can on the ground between the street and fence on the dirt area and it appeared full. We walked around to the small gate and walked inside and approaching the area and we saw empty beer cans and evidence where some individuals had been hiding behind the wall.

We came to the conclusion that the individuals had seen us from a distance while we were checking the other businesses with our spotlights and decided to exit the bar and in going out through the back door, they set off the alarm. Not having any where close by to hide, they ran across the street and jumped the fence and were hiding there waiting for us to leave. Apparently, they were discussing what to do and while they waited, they drank some beer they had stolen from the bar. At some point they got tired of waiting so they left by walking through the cemetery.

So, the noises were explainable, it was not something supernatural or whatever. However, I always wondered if we had decided that night to check out the area and had confronted the individuals. For sure they would have gotten rabbit blood and taken off running. The only direction would have been towards the middle of the cemetery in the dark and I wondered, would I have chases them running through all those graves?

Printed in the United States
by Baker & Taylor Publisher Services